The Irish
Bed & Breakfast
Book

The Irish
Bed & Breakfast
Book

THIRD EDITION

Country and Tourist Homes
Farms • Guesthouses • Inns

By Frank and Fran Sullivan

PELICAN PUBLISHING COMPANY
GRETNA 1998

First edition, September 1994
   Second printing, May 1995
Second edition, July 1996
Third edition, January 1998

The word "Pelican" and the depiction of a pelican are trademarks
of Pelican Publishing Company, Inc.,
and are registered in the U.S. Patent and Trademark Office.

ISBN 1-56554-313-0

Illustrations by Linda Lewis, Jessica Dominguez, Ellen S. Taylor, and Fran Sullivan

Front cover: The Villa (Dublin), border illustration by Ellen Sullivan Taylor

Information in this guidebook is based on authoritative data available at the time of printing. Prices listed are subject to change without notice. Readers are asked to take this into account when consulting this guide.

Manufactured in the United States of America
Published by Pelican Publishing Company, Inc.
1101 Monroe Street, Gretna, Louisiana 70053

*We dedicate this book to our
great-grandparents
who emigrated to America in the 1800s
and carried with them
"a bit of the old sod"—*

*Michael J. and Julia Flannery
and
Michael Patrick and Mary Sullivan*

Contents

Northern Ireland

Acknowledgments

We wish to thank Rebecca Price for her extraordinary work in preparing the new edition and handling the computer/word processing tasks so efficiently. Also, we would like to thank our friends in Ireland who operate B&Bs for their advice on current trends in Ireland. Much of the success of this book is due to their judgment on how the book could better serve the traveling public and be consistent with the realities of operating a bed and breakfast or other lodgings in Ireland. These are the Town and Country Home Association Chairman, Vera Feeney, in Spiddal, County Galway; Dympna Casey, past president, Mulligar, County Westmeath; Cecilia Kiely, Blarney, County Cork; Helen Sheehan, Kilkenny Town; and especially Eileen Kelly, Clontarf, County Dublin. Eileen has generously helped us in many ways over the years.

The Republic of Ireland

IRELAND

Introduction to the Republic of Ireland

BACKGROUND

Ireland is a land of outstanding beauty, serenity, and mystical charm. Its people and land have been propelled through history by dramatic and devastating events. Yet, the people possess a wonderful personality that is loving, kind, friendly beyond compare, hospitable, devout, infectiously fun-loving, witty, and always ready to tease or crack a joke.

When one decides to travel abroad in a foreign land, one must ask the question—why Ireland? How is it different from Sweden, France, England, or other countries you are considering for a visit, assuming that cost is not a factor? In other words, what's there to see and do?

Ireland is probably one of the most beautiful countries in Europe for scenery; it is one of the best for modern and traditional music, theater, and modern and early Christian art; it has an endless chain of castles and historic sites that date back to 4000-3000 B.C.; and the warm and boundless "welcoming" of its people certainly sets it apart from all other countries.

As Irish-Americans who have recently come to love the land and its people, we would say that beneath the tourist veneer exists a more fascinating land and culture than we had ever imagined or proclaimed by most travel books and brochures. As we worked on this book, we both deepened our understanding of Irish history and culture, and in our writing endeavored to provide the reader with enough information for his or her discovery of the Ireland beneath the surface.

Since Ireland is a relatively small country, you might expect the population to be homogeneous, but this is not so. The people of Donegal and those of the South like those found in Kerry and Cork are quite different. The land, many have said before, fashions the character of the people. This is certainly in evidence when you meet the industrious, more serious and somber, yet sincere people of the northwest counties and compare them with the jovial, casual, softer people of the southwest.

This travel book is meant to be a guide for you to design your own itinerary. You should read up on Irish history and the various sights you want to see and then factor in the number of days or weeks you have for your trip, and with the help of a good map, like Michelin's or Bartholemew's, plan an itinerary. Some good references to help you prepare for your trip include:

Rambles in Ireland, by Monie Begley, Devin-Adair Co., Old Greenwich, CT, 1985 (still a great book on Irish culture and history; fascinating writer);

Ireland, World Book Encyclopedia, Field Enterprises Ed. Corp., Chicago and London;

Ireland: A History, by Robert Kee, Abacus Edition, Sphere Books, Ltd., 1982 (excellent but hard to acquire, since it is published in England; published as a result of a special BBC series);

A History of Ireland, by Edmund Curtis, Routledge, 6th Edition, 1961 (the favorite of many historians and general readers).

Francis Bacon's advice still holds true about travel: study the country before you go, read about its culture and history while you're there, and reflect and continue your study when you return.

When planning your trip, a good rule to follow is to allow two nights at each bed and breakfast so you don't get dizzy living out of a suitcase. If you stay only one night at a B&B, it seems like you're on a merry-go-round. You come in at night and leave the next day after breakfast and you get to the point that your days are in the car and the nights in the B&B, without ever getting to know any B&B owners, seeing any local sights, or taking advantage of the many local recreational facilities and special events.

We recommend observing the **Two-Day Rule.** Sometimes you will land at a gem of a place that tickles your fancy and want to stay longer. Don't be so rigid in your plans that you miss the unexpected pleasures of a new town or region like a country fair, a market day, or special musical or dance performance. Have a plan but stay flexible. If you travel in the shoulder season, spring and fall, you won't have to worry so much about booking ahead. But if you travel in the summer, the best B&Bs, those recommended in travel guides, will fill up early.

The Irish Tourist Board, Bord Fáilte, has offices in major cities around the world. In the U.S. it is located at 345 Park Avenue, New York, N.Y. 10154. Telephone: (800) 223-6470 in the U.S. and Canada,

(212) 418-0800, and FAX: (212) 371-9052. In London call, 071-493-3201, and in Sydney, (02) 232-7177. They offer free guides, maps, and information booklets for almost any travel requirements or interests. Some of their guides are the *Town and Country Homes Association: Guest Accommodation* for the current year, with a B&B listing of homes providing reasonable lodgings; *Farm Holidays in Ireland,* with a listing of farm B&Bs; and the *Hotels and Guesthouses—Illustrated Guide—Be Our Guest,* for the more expensive accommodations. Be forewarned that they are not rated or graded. All that the Irish Tourist Board guides give you are the number of rooms, prices, addresses, facilities available, attractions in the area, etc., but not any rating. One does not really know if they are super places or the run of the mill. Some places have the same prices, but vary enormously in charm and value.

That's where this book comes in handy. It will allow you to stay at the best ones! The places in our book were carefully selected to give you the best lodgings in an area—that is, the ones with ambience, charm, cleanliness, hospitable hosts, good facilities and accommodations, and good value for your travel dollar. They were visited by us after being recommended by other travelers, other B&B operators, and travel agents.

Please remember that B&Bs or guesthouses change hands and owners retire, or the quality of the accommodations changes from when we visited them. Also, the prices may change. We have tried to select only those that have all the qualities above but have staying power as well. You will find descriptions of B&Bs, town and country homes, small hotels, guesthouses, and farm B&Bs. Write us at the publisher's address with your comments—good or bad. We would love to hear from you about our listings and any new ones you could recommend for the next edition.

GUARANTEE OF STANDARDS

Bord Fáilte is the official guarantor of minimum standards for most inns, guesthouses, country homes, farmhouses, and town houses. They establish the maximum allowable rate per person, whether couples or single persons. We chose to publish only nightly rates per person for couples (which in Ireland is called the rate for "sharing"). Unless it is stated to be a double rate or the price of the room, you can determine the double or couple rate by multiplying the rate we list by two. Singles pay a higher rate if they are alone. Travel vouchers you may have obtained in an Aer Lingus package or from a travel agent are good for a standard room, one with shared bath.

Most hosts will charge an additional fee of a few pounds for a private bath, accommodations that the Irish call "a room sharing with shower/toilet en suite." In this book, "private bath" means shower, sink, and toilet unless otherwise indicated. A shared bath, usually larger than the private baths, will often have a tub, shower, sink, and toilet. Weekend and weekly rates are sometimes available at substantial savings. A weekend rate includes two nights, two breakfasts, and a Saturday-night dinner. Inquire of the host when you make your reservation as to these special arrangments, and always notify the host in advance if you have special dietary requirements for breakfast. Evening dinner is usually reserved by noon. In many locations, the dinner at the B&B is better than you can find at the local restaurant. Those hosts who have won a Galtee Breakfast Award are especially proud of their home-cooked evening meals as well.

B&Bs displaying the green shamrock sign are those that are inspected and approved by the Bord Fáilte. You can be assured of minimum standards. They are contracted to maintain certain standards and rent for approved rates. All B&Bs listed have been inspected by us and the host(s) interviewed, or have been identified by other owners and/or other experienced travelers as outstanding lodgings—usually both. The B&Bs in our *Irish Bed and Breakfast Book* are held to our required high standards. Please write us with your compliments or suggestions, or if you find that any of the lodgings listed here do not meet your expectations.

PRACTICAL MATTERS

Getting There

Flying to Shannon or Dublin airports directly means your choices are narrowed to **Aer Lingus** (1-800-223-6537) from Boston, Chicago, or New York; **Aeroflot** (1-800-867-8774) from Washington, D.C., Miami, and Chicago; or **Delta** (1-800-241-4141) from Atlanta and New York City. You can also book a charter flight contracted by private associations and organizations such as the Ancient Order of Hibernians (AOH), Irish cultural groups, and such. Check to see if a membership fee is added on to the price of the ticket. Check in the telephone directory if you are near a large city that has a large Irish-American population, and make an inquiry about their charters. Otherwise, inquire of your local travel agent. A good travel agent can advise you about the reputation of most charter companies. We have traveled on Aer Lingus and American Trans Air (ATA) Charter. The charter was cheaper, but the flight was delayed and seats were smaller.

Usually a travel agent's voucher will be good for what the Irish call a "standard" room, one having a shared bath. In some cases you will be asked for a small supplemental fee of a pound or two to cover the cost of the private bath. One package, the Irish Heritage package, includes the services of the Irish Genealogical Research Society.

Genealogical Searches

Millions of Irish were forced to leave their homeland because of the devastation of the famine and other deprivations to seek out a better life in Australia, the United States, or Argentina. You may be descended from these hearty and valiant Irish immigrants who survived these desperate days and you return to Ireland in much different circumstances as tourists and travelers. If you are, it is fun and very satisfying to investigate your roots and possibly find living relatives. In planning your trip you might wish to avail yourself of a registered genealogist to assist you, so that you can set aside time to check archives and records and visit the appropriate ancestral sites. There are many. We can recommend an excellent genealogist: Mrs. Helen Kelly. Her mailing address is Celtic Heritage, 30 Harlech Crescent, Clonskeagh, Dublin 14, Ireland. Her e-mail address: kellyfam@iol.ie.

She and Francis Dowling have produced an excellent instructional tape for the more aggressive, do-it-yourselfers. It is very informative and leads you step by step through the process of a genealogical search. We found it educational in many ways but particularly in the sense that it explained a great deal about the geopolitical structure of early Ireland. You might want to purchase this tape, *Searching for Your Ancestors in Ireland,* produced by Shoreway Video, Int. Ltd. The tape is playable on Canadian and U.S. videocassette recorders and is available at the same address above.

Using the Internet

You can access the Irish Tourist Board's website at http://www.ireland.travel.ie. There you will find additional valuable information on getting there, where to stay, and recreational and current cultural events. However, don't expect to find a rating system for bed and breakfasts or as much detail as in our book; it is simply a good, additional tool for planning.

Money and Changing Currency

Traveler's checks are the best way to carry large sums of money. You can get free traveler's checks if you belong to one of the state AAA clubs. Just remember to bring cash to their office when you purchase their American Express checks. Checks or credit cards are not usually accepted.

When you change money in Ireland, do so at a regular commercial bank, like the Bank of Ireland, and you will get the best exchange rate. Avoid the Dublin or Shannon airport branches as they are usually a little higher than downtown in the nearby city. If you change a little money at the airport to get by for a day or two then do your big exchange in the city branch, you will do better.

B&Bs that accept credit cards are indicated in this book in the full listings. Always ask the host if they accept cards, because we found that credit-card payment is becoming more popular with Irish B&Bs. About a third of town and country home B&Bs use them. Credit-card payment in restaurants and lodgings is a convenient way to handle your money problems. The exchange rate at the date of service is usually quite favorable, and it helps you avoid carrying a lot of cash, especially in Dublin, which has a high incidence of petty theft.

Transportation

Rental Cars

Rent your car before you arrive in Ireland. It is much cheaper. Find a reliable car-rental company through your travel agent. The agent will prebook your car with a partial payment to secure the reservation.

Be sure to check with your credit-card company as to the exact insurance coverage they provide when you wave the collision damage (CDW/LDW): which kind of cars are covered and for what time period. This is extremely important. If you have MasterCard, they will only cover you for 15 days; VISA is currently 30 days. If you rent a car with your MasterCard for 16 days or more, you are not covered at all. Read the fine print in your credit-card brochure describing the services and benefits. If your car is totalled because of this oversight, and you have waived the car company's collision damage, you will pay for a new car replacement out of your pocket. In addition, be forewarned that rental agencies overseas are not regulated by U.S. law so be sure to rent only from companies that have a reliable track record. Your travel agent can advise you which ones are reputable.

Warning: in Dublin, be careful to read fine print on parking meters, as in many districts they need streets clear for commuter traffic, and if you are still parked there after 4 P.M. you may get towed, as we did, to the tune of a $100 fine.

And another thing: in Ireland you must drive on the left side of the road.

Buses

You can take the train to the major provincial cities, and stay in city B&Bs or inns/guesthouses. However, most of the charming B&Bs

are country homes and "using the buses, sometimes you can't get there from here" as they say in Maine. The country bus systems are not very handy due to their odd schedules and frequent stops. If you are lucky to find a main route, they're fine. But check bus schedules carefully. You might take a country bus ride and it might be two days later that you can catch the return. We had to hitchhike once on the Dingle Peninsula to get to where we were going because of the strange routing and schedules of buses. Fran found bus travel fun and adventurous.

When in the big cities or when tour buses are available in the country like in the Dingle or Connemara regions, leave your car in the parking garage ("car park") and take the bus. This allows you to take a rest from driving on the left side and to enjoy the ride and sights without aggravation, and your higher perch lets you see over the hedgerows and stone walls. In Dublin and Cork especially, take the bus because the one-way streets and congestion can drive you mad.

City buses are numbered and only pick up at signs marked with their number. Knowing which number bus to catch is a little bit of a hassle, but the drivers are friendly and usually helpful. But move quickly, for bus doors open and close faster that any we've traveled on in Europe.

Weather

The climate in Ireland is like New England, but with a milder winter, not much snow, and the summers are usually cooler. You can count on rain showers whenever you go. Remember this is a small island set in the Atlantic, and ocean storms blow in quickly with intermittent rainstorms. Fortunately, they move out as quickly.

We found that layering clothing is a good technique for such a variable weather pattern. Put on light clothing, and then add a light wool sweater and rainproof jacket or coat. This way you can adjust to the weather as it changes from cool mornings to very mild or warm temperatures at noon.

Booking Ahead

Booking Outside Ireland

Book ahead for the first night after arrival and the first night before departure, preferably within a short drive from the airport. We like the towns of Ennis, Bunratty, and Adare for a Shannon departure, and Malahide, Clontarf, Drumcondra, Swords, or another North Dublin suburb for a Dublin Airport departure. They are close to the airports and also have excellent restaurants nearby, lower rates, and high quality.

You will find many excellent B&Bs in this book that describe how close they are to the international airports. Book these rooms by calling from outside Ireland. In the U.S. dial 1, then 011 (the international code for both MCI and AT&T), then 353 (the country code), then the number listed in our book (but drop the 0 in the city/town code). You will be surprised that no advanced payment nor credit-card charge is usually required to hold a room. The Irish are very trusting in this regard, and we urge you to cancel well in advance if your travel plans change.

Booking Inside Ireland

Booking ahead within the country only requires you to call the telephone numbers listed and tell the host when you will be arriving. You may ask directions, although we have provided directions. We find that rehearsing and/or recording the directions over the phone is advisable because some are off in the country, up a maze of rural roads. Many hosts are willing to book ahead for you at no charge if you ask their help. We have found this practice to be quite reliable.

General Information about Lodgings

Rooms

Rooms in private homes are often, but not always, small, though cozy with personal touches and pretty decor. Houses built expressly to run a bed and breakfast have plenty of space in the bedrooms, lounges, and dining rooms. Also, the manor homes have large rooms with high ceilings and afford a special treat not only in spaciousness but in Old-World ambience. These features are pointed out in this book in the text of the listing. However, in the country homes or older homes we have sought out those whose hosts are especially warm and genuinely friendly. We feel the warmth of the welcome far outweighs the size consideration of the rooms.

Meals

After checking in, you probably will be offered tea or coffee. The Irish tea is better than the coffee because often the coffee is instant. When you arrive, remind the host of any dietary requirements you may have, and if you want dinner, assuming you arrive early in the afternoon. Better yet, if you book ahead, indicate at that time that you would like dinner. This is a good idea if you are staying in a remote area where there aren't any restaurants nearby, or you are driving a good distance and you don't want to get back in the car again after you arrive.

A full *Irish Breakfast* in this book always consists of eggs cooked to order, bacon, sausage, toast or homemade brown bread with farm-fresh Irish butter or jam (you have to ask for margarine), juice, dry cereal, and tea or coffee. Extras that might be offered are fresh fruit in season, fruited yogurt, cheeses, porridge or oatmeal, scones and/or other baked goods. Special extras that we are finding more and more are French toast or pancakes with syrup, smoked salmon or other fish. The portions are generous. Ask when breakfast is served, and ask for a call if you don't have a travel clock. If you have to leave early to catch a plane or train, your host will usually prepare toast and coffee for you upon request. Irish hosts are very accommodating.

If you want a vegetarian or continental breakfast, let them know the night before and they will probably provide you with the fruited yogurt, toast, fresh fruit, hot or cold cereal, muesli, and tea or coffee. The healthy eating pattern recently popular in America is catching on in Ireland, too.

Booking Tours and Events

Your host will help you book plays, Irish football matches (soccer), fishing trips, horseback riding, and all the other recreational activities in the area. If you ask your host's advice, he/she sometimes will call ahead for you. If not, get the telephone number and use the B&B's box phone, which requires 20-30p to get started. In Dublin, get the *Irish Times* or one of the tabloids and you can find advertisements for the plays and musicals. The Abbey Theatre is Ireland's national repertory company, offering plays by Ireland's best. One night at a Dublin pub with music is a special treat, such as the Abbey Tavern in Howth or Slattery's on Capel Street. The show at Jury's Hotel is elaborate and very enjoyable. Your host(s) can direct you.

Telephoning in Ireland

This can be a problem for Americans who are used to easy access and fast service. Telephoning is very different in Ireland.

There are two ways you can call inside Ireland: with coins, or with a CALLCARD (or Phonecard). CALLCARDS are purchased in local shops and post offices. They are available with so many calling units for so many Irish pounds. We used 20-unit cards and found them far superior to paying with coins. You use the CALLCARD at a telephone booth marked with a yellow band and with the *Card Phone* sign. You just put your card in the slot as indicated and dial the number. The decreasing units are indicated on a digital monitor. One unit is equal to about 20p. When you call long distance, your units will decrease much more rapidly then for local calls. Don't be surprised at the number of phone booths out of order, especially in the countryside.

When you call from your B&B, inn, or guesthouse, you can make local calls for 20 or 30p. The amount for an initial call is indicated in the digital window. Many B&Bs now have coin box telephones near the front door. You dial the number, listen for the dial tone to change when the person answers, then you put in the coin. The remaining time is indicated on a digital clock, and you put more coins in, 10p or better, when time runs out.

Phone calls from hotel rooms have a 200-300 percent surcharge. Be forewarned!

Laundry

We find packing clothes for five days and taking dirty clothes to the laundry is the best way to avoid a lot of heavy luggage.

Except for one B&B in our book (Vera Feeney's in Spiddal), you need to take your laundry to a local laundromat to wash and dry your clothes. Because time is of a premium, we leave our clothes and pay to have them to be washed, dried, and folded. There is only a small additional charge for this. In inns and large guesthouses, they will send them out for you and put the charge on your bill. You send out one day and usually get them back the next. We like to deliver our clothes directly as it speeds up the process and is less expensive.

Northern Ireland

Information on practical matters for Northern Ireland can be found in that section, later in this book.

Having visited the Irish Republic and Northern Ireland, we found the people in both countries to be open, generous, intelligent, and interested in other people. Many have innate wisdom. Other enduring qualities are their humility and kindness. Seldom will you meet an arrogant Irishman or one who would hurt your feelings knowingly. They like to know about your life, your story, and tell you about theirs, spiced with a little humor, and they'll go way back to ancestors.

Security

In the larger cities, such as Cork, Galway, and especially Dublin, be sure to leave nothing of value that can be seen inside your car while it is parked on the street. Lock cameras, suitcases, and shopping bags in your trunk out of view. Those B&Bs that have a locked car park off the street are much preferred in Dublin. Unfortunately, in Dublin, as in other big cities where tourists congregate, there has been a high incidence of thefts. So be careful to keep wallets in your deeper front pockets, and wear no pocketbook slung over your shoulder but carry it in front with one arm over it. One option is to buy a waist purse or fanny pack that straps around your body. Travel in pairs or larger groups if possible.

Country Carlow

County Carlow presents you with soft rolling hills and lush pasture-land. Two important rivers run through it, the Barrow and the Slaney, which give great opportunities for avid anglers. Fish to your heart's content for pike, trout, or salmon or do "coarse" fishing. The lovely Mount Leinster is good for hiking; it is part of the Blackstairs Mountains along the southeast border. Near the center of the county is Ballymoon Castle. Peaceful Carlow is only an hour away from busy Dublin for a getaway vacation. It is close to Glendalough in County Wicklow, and only 10 to 15 miles away from exciting Kilkenny.

Laburnum Lodge
Anne Byrne
Bunclody Road N81
Tullow, County Carlow
Telephone: 0503-51718
Bedrooms: 4, all with private baths.
Rates: £17 p.p. with bath; 25 percent discount for children under 12.
Vouchers accepted. **Credit cards:** None. **Open:** March 1 to October
30. **Children:** All ages. **Pets:** In the shed. **Smoking:** No. **Provision for
handicapped:** Yes. **Directions:** There are signs posted. From the bridge
in Tullow, take the N81 towards Dublin and Laburnum Lodge will be
1 mile up on the right.

This lovely new Georgian home is in the beautiful Tullow Valley surrounded by mountains. Anne is cheerful and outgoing and like a
breath of fresh air. There is a feeling of bringing the outside in as
there are lots of large windows, and the sliding glass doors in her dining room open onto her award-winning gardens. The handsomely
decorated sitting room has bold, dark-blue drapes and cream walls
and the bedrooms have unusual colors such as lemon, pink, and rose.
Her Irish Breakfast includes choice of eggs or French toast, and fruit,
yogurt, and cheeses. We can attest to her very tasty fresh scones, which
we smelled baking as we entered. On a getaway weekend here you'll
have access to fishing, golf (18 holes at Mount Wolseley), hunting,
river cruising, signposted walks, and visits to Altamount Gardens. You
may visit the Brown's Hill Dolmen Stones or even go hang gliding
nearby. Anne's brother, Jim O'Toole, wrote a book on manor houses
in County Carlow.

County Cavan

County Cavan has an odd shape, like a paramecium. The tail is sandwiched between Fermanagh and Leitrim, the head towards Monaghan, the Meaths, and Longford. It is a county of picturesque farms, lakes, and the Erne and Annalee rivers. There are many good lakes for fishing, especially Lough Erne and Lough Oughter above Cavan and Butlers Bridge. This is a particularly pretty area to see. The Derragarra Inn, an award-winning pub at Butlers Bridge, has good, reasonable meals. There is a Folk Museum just across the street from it. Cavan is a bustling town with Cavan Crystal and several singing pubs. Visit Killykeen Forest Park not far from Cavan, with the ruins of Lough Oughter Castle and nature trails, swimming, and fishing. You can rent a forest chalet here by the week.

In the south of Cavan is the lovely, quiet town of Virginia amidst miles of rolling green hills, much resembling our state of Virginia. Flowers and farms abound and it borders on Lough Ramor with 22 islands in it. The lake is part of the town and adds much to its special beauty. North of Virginia is another small town known for its mention in a well-known Irish ditty. This town, Ballyjamesduff, is worth a visit. County Cavan is known for its golf and for being a crossroads.

Hilltop Farm B&B
Elizabeth Dunne
Belturbet, County Cavan
Telephone: 049-22114
Bedrooms: 10; all with private baths.
Rates: £16-17 p.p.; Single £5 extra; 20 percent discount for children under 12. Vouchers accepted. **Credit cards:** VISA, MasterCard, Eurocard. **Open:** All year. **Children:** All ages. **Pets:** No. **Smoking:** Yes, but not in dining room. **Provision for handicapped:** Yes, through the kitchen. **Directions:** From Cavan take the N3; farm is exactly three miles from Butlers Bridge on the right.

This fairly new house is an actual farmhouse as Mrs. Dunne's son runs a steer and sheep farm in the back. Mr. and Mrs. Dunne will greet you with tea. They have four ladies who help run the B&B, which has clean comfortable rooms, all with pink and beige covers and cream or lilac walls. All baths are carpeted. There are sinks in every room, and the halls are stenciled. The living room has a marble fireplace, and the dining room is huge with views of the lake, which is famous for fishing. People come from all over Europe to fish here. She packs a lunch, serves fantastic evening meals, and is always ready with a cup of tea for travelers. Her Irish Breakfast includes a selection of cereals. There are also activities like golf, river cruising, cycling, and walking tours right in the town of Belturbet.

Halcyon
Brid and Walter Myles
Drumalee
Cavan, County Cavan
Telephone: 049-31809; **FAX:** 049-62531
Bedrooms: 5; 4 with private baths, 1 with shared.
Rates: £16 p.p. private bath; £14 p.p. shared bath; Single £18; 20 percent discount for children under 12. £12 dinner on request. **Credit cards:** Yes. **Open:** January 8 to December 18. **Children:** All ages. **Pets:** Yes. **Smoking:** Yes, but not in dining room. **Provision for handicapped:** Yes. **Directions:** Beyond the Roman Catholic Cathedral on the N3 take the Cootehill Road. At first crossroads, turn right and Halcyon is 100 yards up that road on the left side.

This cozy bungalow is family run and Walt and Brid will greet you; they are very personable and helpful. Their genealogical library and books on Irish history are in the lounge. This is where you get your welcome tea and share the family TV. They'll give you lots of guidance on ancestral tracing, hiking in the area, and trips around Ireland. We really enjoyed their conversation. The lounge has many lovely original Irish paintings. The large garden and conservatory is for guest use. The dining room is spacious and Walt does the cooking. The bedrooms are well organized with huge towels and facecloths. One room is decorated in antique white linen and lace, one is cream and pale green, another is cream with navy-striped duvets. The front room is rose and white. The bungalow's good central location puts you very close to the Cavan Sports Centre, the Equestrian Centre, an 18-hole golf club with special fees available, and fishing. The hosts have discounts for Cavan Crystal. Dinner is available on request.

ALSO RECOMMENDED

Cavan Town, *Lisnamandra,* Bert and Iris Neill, Crossdoney. Telephone: 049-37196. Bedrooms: 6, 4 with private baths. Spacious period residence on dairy farm. Situated 7 km south of Cavan on Killesdandra Road. Lots of amenities. Won Galtee award for breakfasts. Recommended by May Herity of Letterkenny, County Donegal.

Cavan Town, *Oakdene,* Ann and Paddy Gaffney, 29 Cathedral Rd. Telephone: 049-31698. Bedrooms: 4, all with shared baths. Recommended by Brid Myles of Cavan Town.

County Clare

County Clare's most important feature is that it contains Shannon Airport, where everyone enters the Irish Republic who wants to see the West Coast. So that will be our starting place. If you head south toward Limerick, you'll have to see the Bunratty Castle and Folk Park. If you make reservations for the Medieval Banquet at Bunratty Castle, you'll encounter quite a wild party. If you'd like to see bright costumes, music, performers, and storytellers; try some genuine mead; and try eating a big meal with only a knife—all amidst a huge hall full of people from every country you can imagine—then you'll have a jolly, even hilarious evening. Durty Nelly's, a pub next door, is a fun place to do your first Irish singing, but it's a bit seedy.

Lough Derg and the River Shannon form the eastern edge of the county. The lengthy river finally meets the sea at the southern edge, forming a narrow bay. Killaloe, a town at the base of Lough Derg, has water-skiing, sailing, and a riverboat tour of the lake. Also, visit the 12th-century St. Flannan's Cathedral and Ogham Stone there.

If you head northwest, you'll come to Ennis, a busy little town with a marketplace, good B&Bs, restaurants, and many singing pubs. There is a castle at Knappogue in Quin, and the Dromoland Castle is almost into Ennis. Surrounding Ennis are pretty, peaceful farmlands. From Ennis, travel north to Lahinch via the N85, which passes through Ennistymon, or go by the R476 and visit Corofin first, a good freshwater fishing spot. Here you will find the Clare Heritage Centre with lots of information for Clare genealogy seekers.

Lahinch is an interesting seaside resort with shops, quaint cafés, beaches, and lovely sea views. Horses graze on the green cliffs above the beach. To the south of here, you'll find surfing beaches at Spanish Point and the spot where ships of the Spanish Armada were wrecked. Farther south on the sea is Kilkee, with some gorgeous cliff scenery.

The most fascinating steep cliffs of fame are the Cliffs of Moher, dropping down to the sea just outside Liscannor. The cliffs are worth a look in all kinds of weather except thick fog. They are hauntingly dramatic, moss green in summer and gold-brown in fall. From the Cliffs, travel north to Doolin on the coast, where you may catch a ferry to the Aran Islands. There used to be an old custom for Aran Island boys to row over to Doolin on a specified day each year to seek a bride. Next you'll want to see the Burren, a natural geological wonder of stark, rocky hills that hold unique wildflowers, animal life, and mystical springs. You can take a walk through with a guide if you book ahead. Ask at Lisdoonvarna or Ballyvaughan. See the Aillwee Caves, too, with many stalactites and a Tea Room for a snack.

Bunratty Lodge
Mary Browne
Bunratty, County Clare
Telephone: 061-369402; **FAX:** 061-369363
Bedrooms: 6, all with private baths.
Rates: £18 p.p.; Single £30; 20 percent discount for children under 12.
Vouchers not accepted. **Credit cards:** Yes. **Open:** Mid-March to
November 1. **Children:** Yes, 7 years and older. **Pets:** No. **Smoking:** No.
Provision for handicapped: Yes. **Directions:** Coming from Shannon
Airport (on the N18), after about 4 miles take side road to Bunratty
Castle, sign on left. Then take road on left between Bunratty Castle
and Durty Nelly's pub. Go 1½ miles to intersection. Bunratty Lodge
is two-story blue home across the intersection in country settting.

Bunratty Lodge is stunning inside and out, a stately neo-Georgian
modern home painted blue and trimmed in white surrounded by a
well-kept garden and gated entrance. The living room is spacious and
elegant with a blue rug, white fireplace, and beautiful flowered drapes.
The bedrooms are pink and grey, green and pink, with a myriad of
flowered designs and all with thick, fluffy quilts. All the spacious bedrooms have color TVs and large tiled baths with towel heaters. Besides
the full Irish Breakfast, your gracious hostess, Mary Browne, serves a
choice of eggs and potatoes, fruit, yogurt and cheeses, and an option
of French toast. She has received the Galtee county award for her
breakfasts. The dining room is comfortable and well lighted with large
windows to the garden and a choice of large table or separates.
Medieval banquets at the nearby Bunratty Castle can be arranged,
along with other advice on touring this area. Golf, horseback riding,
swimming in the heated pool at Shannon-Shamrock Hotel, fishing,
or a visit to the Folk Park behind the Castle, followed by a pint at the
famous Durty Nelly's pub, are some of the local features.

Clover Hill Lodge
Anne Nash
Bunratty, County Clare
Telephone: 061-369039; **FAX:** 061-360520
Bedrooms: 4, all with private baths.
Rates: £17 p.p.; Single £26. Vouchers accepted. **Credit cards:** Yes.
Open: April 1 to October 31. **Children:** Yes. **Pets:** No. **Smoking:** No.
Provision for handicapped: Yes. **Directions:** Coming from Shannon
Airport, take the N18 for 4 miles. Take the side road to Bunratty Castle, sign on the left. At Bunratty Castle, take a sharp left. Pass the Bunratty Folk Park, and drive up sign posted road for about ¼ miles.
House is on left.

This modern, red brick, dormered house is situated right between
Bunratty Castle and Durty Nelly's, so it is easy to find. Anne will very
helpful to you in finding the airport, only 10 minutes away, as well as
other places of interest. Her rooms are beautifully decorated and all
have orthopedic mattresses, TVs, and hairdryers. Anne gives you a
choice of breakfasts from a menu. They include juice, cereal, all-Irish
fresh fruit with lowfat organic yogurt, ham slices with Irish cheese
and fruit, poached or scrambled eggs, pancakes and maple syrup,
along with filtered coffee, herb teas, or hot chocolate. Try the
medieval dinner and show at Bunratty Castle. It is lots of fun—you'll
get a glass of mead, and you will be served very good period-style food
while being entertained by a beautiful group of young people in
period costumes. Durty Nelly's is a good pub for singing and trying
Guinness stout or a good pub snack. This area gives you an early rest
after your flight and easy access to the Cliffs of Moher and coast or
south to County Kerry.

Rockfield House
Margaret Garry
Hill Road
Bunratty, County Clare
Telephone and **FAX:** 061-364391
Bedrooms: 6, all with private baths.
Rates: £16 p.p.; Single £25; 20 percent discount for children under 12.
Vouchers accepted. **Credit cards:** Yes. **Open:** All year, except Christmas
week. **Children:** All ages. **Pets:** No. **Smoking:** No. **Provision for handicapped:** No. **Directions:** As you approach Bunratty Village, make a
left turn after Avoca Handweavers just before Fitzpatricks Bunratty
Shamrock Hotel. You will find Rockfield House about 300 yards up
that windy road on the righthand side. There are two white eagles on
the entrance gates.

Beside being in the midst of all the Bunratty sights and activities,
this is a very pleasant and modern home hosted by a very friendly and
warm Mrs. Garry. One bedroom has a balcony and view of River Shannon. All bedrooms are pink and green and have TVs, tea and coffee,
hairdryers, and electric blankets. A trouser press is in the hallway.
Being perched on a peaceful hillside with the modern decor, it
reminds one of California and commands a panoramic view of the
River Shannon. However, the Irish wit and charm, bright and cheery
rooms, and the tasty breakfast will let you know you are enjoying the
best of the Irish Republic. Great brewed coffee is served along with
your tasty cooked breakfast. You may choose a delicious continental or
vegetarian one. All are served in a beautiful dining room that has a
light green theme with lace tablecloths. A lounge with TV can be
enjoyed with coffeee or tea upon request. Fishing at Six-Mile Bridge,
golf, swimming at the nearby hotel, or visits to nearby Bunratty Castle
and Folk Park and Durty Nelly's can be arranged by Mrs. Garry. Let
her prebook your night at the Castle banquet.

Massabielle
Monica O'Loughlin
Quin Road
Ennis, County Clare
Telephone: 065-29363
Bedrooms: 5; 4 with private baths, 1 with shared.
Rates: £17 p.p. private bath; £15 p.p. shared bath; Single £18; 20 percent discount for children under 12. Vouchers accepted. **Credit cards:** None. **Open:** April 10 to October 15. **Children:** All ages. **Pets:** No. **Smoking:** In lounge only. **Provision for handicapped:** Yes, rooms on first floor. **Directions:** At Ennis railway station, travel out the Quin Road for 1 mile to sign for Massabielle.

Massabielle is a lovely modern house with gardens in a peaceful country setting just out of the center of Ennis town. It is a good stop (30 minutes) from Shannon Airport for people heading north. The Irish setter, Ross, may greet you and you may see cows nearby. Monica is kind and sweet, as are all her children, who help her. Their warmth and sense of humor pervade the house. The rooms are prettily decorated with lots of pinks and whites and antique wardrobes and dressers. The pleasant living room has a piano, fireplace, and TV and opens to the handsome dining room. Expect a delightful visit from younger children—James, Roisin, Edel, or Claire. Breakfast is typical with additions of fruit and yogurt and homemade muffins. An all-weather tennis court is right on the premises. Bunratty Castle and Folk Park are 20 minutes away. The Burren is 20 minutes north and the beaches of Lahinch are 30 minutes away. Ennis is a bustling county seat and older city and a fun place to visit on Market Day. Golf tuition, horseback riding, and tennis can be arranged.

Sea Haven
Patrick and Eilis Blake
Road to Cliffs of Moher
Liscannor, County Clare
Telephone: 065-81385; **FAX:** 065-81417
Bedrooms: 6, all with private baths.
Rates: £16 p.p.; Single £21; 25 percent discount for children under 12.
Vouchers accepted. £14 reserved dinner. **Credit cards:** None. **Open:**
All year, except Christmas Day. **Children:** All ages. **Pets:** Yes, in garage.
Smoking: Restricted. **Provision for handicapped:** Yes. **Directions:** From
Lahinch, take the road to the Cliffs of Moher. Sea Haven is a white
gabled bungalow on a hill on the right. A big B&B sign is on a gable.

Sea Haven is a lovely house, sitting high enough to have a gorgeous
panoramic view of Liscannor Bay and surrounding farms. The Blakes'
good service and tranquil surroundings make this a special place to
stay. Most of the rooms are large with a floral theme; all have
wardrobes, coffee and tea service, and a view of walled meadows or the
bay. The rooms are peach and pastel with antiques for ambience.
Bathrooms are tiled. The handsomely decorated sitting room has a
fireplace and TV; the dining room is pretty, too, and both have views
of the water. For breakfast, served buffet style, you can have Full Irish,
choice of fruit or juice, brewed coffee, choice of eggs—scrambled,
boiled, fried, or poached—local cheeses, and mackerel or herring in
summer. A dinner can be ordered off the menu of their famous
restaurant, and served at the B&B. The Captain's Deck is built like a
ship and is in the town of Liscannor 5 minutes away. They serve fresh
salmon, sole, lobster, and vegetarian and meat dishes. Nearby features are Cliffs of Moher, all water sports, golf, fishing, horseback riding, caving, and cliff walks.

ALSO RECOMMENDED

Ennis, *Hazeldene House,* Mrs. Ina Troy, Barefields. Telephone: 065-27212. Bedrooms: 4, all en suite with TV. Private parking. Evening meals available. Modern country home on Ennis-Galway road (N18). It's 5 minutes from Ennis Center. Ideal touring base for the Burren, Cliffs of Moher, and Aillwee Caves.

Ennis, *Villa Nova,* Mrs. Mareaid O'Connor, 1 Woodlawn, Lahinch Road. Telephone: 065-28570. Bedrooms: 5, 3 with private baths. Vouchers accepted. Bungalow on N85. Restaurant and pub with music are a 2 minutes' walk.

Kilkee, *Harbour Lodge,* Mrs. Patsy Flanagan, 6 Marine Parade. Telephone: 065-56090. Bedrooms: 4, all with private baths. Town home across from beach in scenic area. Vouchers accepted.

Lahinch, *Mulcarr House,* Mrs. Brid Fawl, Ennistymon Road. Telephone: 065-81123. Bedrooms: 4, 3 private baths. Walking distance to golf and beach. Vouchers accepted. Smoke-free home.

Liscannor, *Moher Lodge,* Mrs. Mary Considine, Cliffs of Moher. Telephone: 064-81269. Bedrooms: 5, 4 with private baths. Spectacular view of valley below.

Lisdoonvarna, *Fernhill Farmhouse,* Tessie Linnane and family, Doolin Road. Telephone: 065-74040. Bedrooms: 6, 4 with private baths. A comfortable 300-year-old farmhouse 2 miles from Doolin village and 2 miles from Lisdoonvarna. Traditional Irish music nightly in Doolin. Recommended by Tim and Chris-Ann Kane of New York.

County Cork

County Cork makes up almost half of Southwest Ireland, so as you can guess, there are vast differences in the terrain. In the north around Mallow, the pastureland is flat and broad with dark-green, low shrubs separating the sheep enclosures. Purple mountains can be seen to the north and west.

Moving south you will come to the town of Blarney first, with its famed Blarney Woolen Mills and the Blarney Castle, which contains the celebrated Blarney Stone. The Blarney Park Hotel nearly always has some kind of Irish music, modern or traditional, along with step dancing or set dancing to watch. Just five or six miles southeast you may visit the largest city of the Southwest, which is Cork City. Most of it sits between the north and south channels of the split Lee River, with its numerous bridges.

Here you may want to take the traditional walk along Patrick Street to the Grand Parade or wander to the edges of the city to catch glimpses of St. Mary's Pro-Cathedral or St. Finn Barre's Cathedral, the Church of St. Peter and St. Paul, or Father Matthew Memorial Church. Peruse the many art galleries and craft centers, museums, and the Cork Opera House, which offers delightful plays, musicals, and operas. We had an excellent meal in the dining room of The Moore's Hotel on Morrison's Island at the south end of town. One memorable night we walked into a small, dark, well-visited pub called "An Bodhran," and found a well-loved young fiddler playing his heart out with other musicians. He played for hours, to our joy. In September and October, look for the famous Cork Film Festival and the Jazz Festival.

Due west of Cork City on the N22 headed toward Killarney and just before a mountain pass is the beautiful medieval town of Macroom, set out in the country. Flowered window boxes abound and an old stone fort graces the town center.

About 16 miles southwest of Cork is the happy seaside town of Kinsale, labeled the Gourmet Capital of Ireland. We just missed a big gourmet competition among the many fine restaurants there on our last visit. It has the good gift shops and coffee shops of a tourist town, but a small place where we had the best soup and sandwich by a peat fire is Mother Hubbard's on Pearse Street.

From here you might want to head out to West Cork on windy little roads along tiny bays that cut into the whole of the Southwest. You'll pass beautiful small villages like Courtmacsherry, Clonakilty, Rosscarbery, and Baltimore, tucked around harbors full of sailboats. On the N71 is the classy town of Skibbereen, which booms in summer; farther west, then north, is Bantry with more formality and sophistication, and a commanding view from its hills of Bantry Bay and the wonderful mountains of the Beara Peninsula beyond.

To the east of Cork City, you'll want to see the charming port of Cobh (pronounced "Cove"), from where most emigrants had to leave by boat in the 1800s for the foreign shores of America. Imposing St. Colman's Cathedral reigns on a hill overlooking the town with its multicolored buildings fronting the harbor. Farther east is the medieval town of Youghal, with remnants of an old town gate and walls, and ancient buildings where Cromwell hid his arms. It has a pretty old lighthouse and farms that stretch out with views of the sea.

Dunauley
Rosemary McAuley
Seskin
Bantry, County Cork
Telephone: 027-50290
Bedrooms: 5, all with private baths; 1 is a self-catering suite.
Rates: £20-22 p.p. private bath; £25 suite; Single £25; 20 percent discount for children. **Credit cards:** None. **Open:** May 1 to September 30.
Children: Yes, 12 or older. **Pets:** No. **Smoking:** No. **Provision for handicapped:** None. **Directions:** From the center of Bantry follow the signs to the hospital. Take the one-way street up the hill. Pass the church on the right. Take the second right. Continue up the hillside road to the Dunauley sign. The B&B is on the right up the driveway. The main entry door is at the back, but car parking is provided in front once unloaded.

This modern country home is elegant and the large, comfortable living room/dining room with fireplace has wraparound bay windows with a most extraordinary panoramic view of all of Bantry Bay and the Beara Peninsula from high atop the hill. The bedrooms are very pretty and spacious. Three rooms upstairs share one large bathroom; two downstairs have private baths. All are tastefully decorated in blue, pink and green, or apricot. One of the downstairs rooms is the honeymoon bedroom. All rooms have tea- and coffee-making facilities. The breakfast menu almost defies description as it excels in most categories from fresh-squeezed orange juice or grapefruit decorated with kiwi fruit, to a trolley of cereals with toppings of raisins and fruit, to omelets with 4 fillings, or smoked salmon and scrambled eggs. Brewed coffee and a variety of teas complement the entrées, not to mention the scones and homemade breads. Extraordinary! Fishing, sailing, golf, walks, and Bantry House are in town 5 minutes away.

Larchwood House
Sheila Vaughan
Pearsons Bridge
Bantry, County Cork
Telephone: 027-66181
Bedrooms: 4, all private baths.
Rates: £25 p.p. Vouchers not accepted. £23-30 dinner. **Credit cards:** Yes. **Open:** All year, except Christmastime. **Children:** Yes, 8 or older. **Pets:** No. **Smoking:** Yes. **Provision for handicapped:** None. **Directions:** On the N17 at Ballylickey, take Kealkill Road for 2 miles, north of Bantry. At Pearsons Bridge on Kealkill Road, take a sharp right. The house is 300 yards on the right.

A rare find is this enchanting "restaurant with rooms." The B&B is part of a small, intimate gourmet restaurant with cooking that has flair and originality. The bedrooms are luxurious, spacious, and beautifully decorated. The dining room overlooks their grand gardens and a small river. For those who like exquisite dining and then a peaceful evening in an elegant bedroom upstairs—instead of a lot of driving—this is the place. The gardens are the handiwork of the husband, Aiden Vaughan, a professional photographer, who has transformed the surroundings, using stone and plants, into an extraordinary, enchanting 6 acres of beauty. Sheila matches his artistry in the culinary department. Breakfast is ordered off a menu and features fresh fruit; eggs any style, some with smoked salmon (typically Irish) or grilled kippered herring; baked fresh haddock; and a local cheese plate. She has been a super chef at the Dromoland Castle. The small lounge provides drinks in a homey atmosphere, or you can take a stroll through the garden down the "39 steps" to a place where the local salmon river becomes a pool. The Vaughans are gracious and will make this an idyllic treat off the beaten path.

Shangri-la
Ursula Schiesser
Glengarriff Road
Bantry, County Cork
Telephone: 027-50244; **FAX:** 027-50244
Bedrooms: 6; 4 with private baths, 2 with shared.
Rates: £18 p.p. private bath; £16 p.p. shared bath; Single £8 extra; 20 percent discount for children under 10. Vouchers accepted. **Credit cards:** All major ones. **Open:** All year, except Christmas week. **Children:** All ages. **Pets:** No. **Smoking:** Restricted. **Provision for handicapped:** No, hillside lot. **Directions:** Coming from town on the N71, the Glengarriff Road, take the first right after ROWA Pharmaceuticals and the first left to enter the car park at the back of the property.

The view from the living room and sun porch is panoramic and beautiful. The rooms are handsomely decorated: one in green and aqua flowers, one with a pink and white canopy, another with an orange and lace canopy. All are fashionable, charming, and comfortable, with coffee- and tea-making facilities. Ms. Schiesser is a delightful host and will make your stay in Bantry a pleasant one. We were enchanted with the story of the first settlers in Ireland, who came ashore in Bantry led by Cessera, a woman captaining the crew of 53. Ask her about the soup field across the street. There is a choice of menu for breakfast. Some different choices are coddled eggs and pancakes as well as cheeses, fruits, and yogurts. The full Irish Breakfast is served in the pretty dining room adjoining the well-appointed living room. All common rooms have views of the water and the garden. Many rooms also have a view of the water. This B&B maintains high standards! Bantry House and Gardens and fishing, sailing, walks, and golf are in the area. In 1996, there was a bicentennial celebration of the French Armada in Bantry Bay.

Brehon House
Adrian and Mary Spillett
Killowen
Blarney, County Cork
Telephone: 021-385047
Bedrooms: 3, all with private baths.
Rates: £17 p.p.; Single £22. Vouchers accepted. 25 percent discount for children under 12. **Credit cards:** None. **Open:** March 1 to October 31. **Children:** All ages. **Pets:** No. **Smoking:** Restricted to sun-room or conservatory. **Provision for handicapped:** None. **Directions:** Pass the Blarney Park Hotel, leaving Blarney. Take second road on the right and keep right for 2 miles. Note the sign to Brehon House with the shamrock 300 yards on the right, near Killowen Garden Centre.

This charming couple will make you feel right at home at this modern house in a quiet, farm-country setting. You will receive welcoming tea and scones. Their guest book overflows with glowing and superlative comments. The dining room has oval tables and fresh flowers. The breakfast is the full Irish Breakfast with homemade sausages and fresh free-range eggs, fruit, yogurt, and cheeses. The dinner is prepared with vegetables from the large garden beside the house. Rooms are cheery and bright, decorated in pretty pinks, blue-greys, and whites with white dressing tables. Two rooms have TV. Bathrooms are modern and tiled. The lounge is comfortable and adequate for this size B&B. The ambience and the hosts make this a great place to stay. Golf and a riding center are nearby, as is Blarney Castle. This is an ideal base for touring the south.

Claragh Bed and Breakfast
Cecilia Kiely
Waterloo Road
Blarney, County Cork
Telephone: 021-886308
Bedrooms: 4, all with private baths.
Rates: £16.50 p.p. private bath; £13.50 p.p. shared bath; Single £18.
Vouchers accepted. **Credit cards:** None. **Open:** April to October. **Children:** No. **Pets:** No. **Smoking:** Restricted. **Provision for handicapped:**
Yes, all rooms on ground level. **Directions:** Follow signs on Waterloo
Road out of Blarney Village to Claragh. About 2 miles out, you'll find
the house on the left.

Cecilia Kiely will surely lighten your visit to the Irish Republic with
her boundless energy and special Irish humor. You are always greeted
with tea and hot scones on your arrival. But the hostess makes your
visit especially warm and friendly with her care in directing you to
the sights and sounds of Blarney and Cork City. Electric blankets are
turned on before you retire. The lounge, although small, is lovely
and adequate for 4 bedrooms, and the dining room allows for separate tables. The rooms are decorated in pink and green, and peach
and green with floral accents. The baths have modern showers with
sinks and toilets. Breakfast has fresh homemade brown bread, fruit,
and yogurts along with a choice of cooked Irish Breakfast. Cecilia features a French toast with syrup that is delicious. The quiet of the countryside will be restful and relaxing after a hard day on the road. This
home is near Blarney center, where you can shop until you drop at
Blarney Woolen Mills and other shops, kiss the Blarney Stone at the
Castle, hear Irish music, dance traditional Irish set dances, or swim at
Blarney Park Hotel. You may want to try to catch the big salmon, as
Frank did (tried, that is). Check out Christie's Restaurant. It's great!

Evergreen House
Mrs. Noreen Curran
Rathpeacon
Blarney, County Cork
Telephone: 021-305715
Bedrooms: 6, all with private baths.
Rates: £16 p.p.; Single £20; 25 percent discount for children. **Credit cards:** None. **Open:** March 1 to October 31. **Children:** All ages. **Pets:** No. **Smoking:** Restricted to lounge. **Provision for handicapped:** Yes.
Directions: From the N20, the Blarney/Cork Road, look for Country Squire, and turn sharply left immediately after it. Go ¼ mile to the sign for Evergreen House and take the first left. It is the 5th house on the right. It is advised because of current road construction to call and ask for changes in directions.

Martin Curran, who was a contractor in Chicago for many years, came back in 1976 to Blarney and his family land to build an extraordinary home overlooking the Valley below. The garden is magnificent and the house is both charming and spacious. The rooms look like pages from *House and Garden*. One room has a brass queen-size bed with a quilted rose pattern on the spread; another large room is in rose and grey. There are views from some bedrooms. One with a peach accent overlooks the garden and has a spacious bathroom with a bidet. Many baths have showers and tubs. The dining room is an elegant gold and yellow and a traditional Irish Breakfast is served with choices from a menu with French toast, yogurts, and fresh fruits. It is a charming place to spend a few days. It is 5 miles to Blarney and 2 miles to Cork City. This house is 1 mile to a golf course and 2 miles to horseback riding. Walk to the Country Squire Restaurant; it's highly recommended.

Inchavara House
Breda O'Dwyer
Stoneview
Blarney, County Cork
Telephone: 021-385549; **FAX:** 021-393796
Bedrooms: 4; 3 with private baths, 1 with shared.
Rates: £16.50-17 p.p. private bath; £14.50-15 p.p. shared bath; Single
£22. Vouchers not accepted. **Credit cards:** None. **Open:** May 1 to
November 1. **Children:** Negotiable. **Pets:** No. **Smoking:** No. **Provision
for handicapped:** None. **Directions:** It is 1 mile outside of Blarney
Village off R617. Off the N20 from Mallow, take the first right turn to
Blarney, go a half-mile, and take the second right; Inchavara House is
on your right.

This lovely country home was recommended to us by a guest in
Dublin, and again by another B&B owner in Blarney, and we are
thrilled to include it. What a delightful home, with a beautiful dining
room and a spacious lounge both opening to a large conservatory or
sun-room with floor-to-ceiling glass, overlooking the beautiful garden
in front and hills and Blarney Castle beyond. It is a great place for having a before-dinner drink or playing cards. The bedrooms are decorated in blues and pinks. There are various room accommodations.
One bedroom with a huge bath is very large, fitted with a double and
a single brass bed. Mrs. O'Dwyer is a congenial and welcoming host.
The breakfast is regular or continental. The regular breakfast includes
a choice of eggs, black pudding, and hot scones to name a few extras.
The buffet of cereals, yogurts, and fruits makes a nice continental one.
The coffee is brewed! In fact tea- and coffee-making facilities are available in the sun-room during the day. Horseback riding and golf can be
found nearby in Blarney.

Hillside Farm
Bella Helen
Kilgarriffe
Clonakilty, County Cork
Telephone: 023-33139
Bedrooms: 4; 2 with private baths, 2 with shared.
Rates: £16 p.p. private bath; £14 shared bath; Single £18; 50 percent discount for children. Vouchers accepted. £12 dinner. **Credit cards:** None. **Open:** March to November. **Children:** All ages. **Pets:** Yes. **Smoking:** No. **Provision for handicapped:** None. **Directions:** To the northwest from Cork, turn right at the Shell station onto Enniskean Road (R588). The farm is 2 miles on the left.

When we were there, pups were being born in the hayloft, new calves were suckling their mothers, chickens, geese, and rare fowl were clucking and calling in the barnyard. This is a 150-acre, living, vibrant dairy farm with all the noises and smells one would expect at a rural homestead. Mrs. Helen served us fresh scones with her own crab-apple jelly (just made) on the side shelf of her old-style kitchen. She gives baking demonstrations. Although rustic, this pink farmhouse B&B has appeal for those who like to visit a working farm. There are fine views from beautifully furnished rooms. The comfortable lounge has antique furniture, and the dining room is attractive. Dinner features 4 courses, with a roast such as leg of lamb or salmon, potato, fresh brown bread, 2 vegetables from the garden, and berry pie. Yum! Breakfast is likewise scrumptious and generous with homemade white pudding, jams, and jellies. It is a great place for young children to learn about farm life. They would never want to leave. This farm is within 45 minutes' drive of Cork Airport and Ringaskiddy Ferryport. There is good bird watching along the estuary.

Belvedere Lodge
Tim and Marie McGrath
Tivoli
Cork City, County Cork
Telephone and **FAX:** 021-501682
Bedrooms: 11, all with private baths.
Rates: £28; Single £5 extra; 50 percent discount for children. Vouchers not accepted. Dinner is offered, inquire about price. **Credit cards:** All major ones. **Open:** All year. **Children:** All ages. **Pets:** No. **Smoking:** Yes. **Provision for handicapped:** Yes. **Directions:** One mile east of Cork City on Dublin/Waterford road just before the corner of Limerick road (north). Silver Springs Hotel is on the opposite corner.

This lovely Victorian guesthouse with wrought iron canopy has spacious and beautifully decorated bedrooms. The elegant curtains and quilts and wall to wall carpeting with fine furniture grace your eyes when you enter the bedrooms. They all have TVs, telephones, and tea- and coffee-making facilities. The beautiful lounge has a Victorian floral decor with marble fireplace and accompanying period furniture. The equally handsome dining room is cranberry with green carpeting and separate tables, all adjoining the patio with a view of the garden. An elaborate breakfast menu includes selection of fresh fruits, fresh-squeezed orange juice, cereals, fresh fish and grills, and scrambled eggs with smoked salmon. There is a private, secure car park. The Belvedere Lodge offers a good base for visiting the sights in Cork City and the surrounding historical and cultural sights of the region. The McGraths can direct you to the recreational facilities as well.

Victoria Lodge
Brendan Long
Victoria Cross
Cork City, County Cork
Telephone: 021-542233; **FAX:** 021-542572
Bedrooms: 30, all with private baths.
Rates: £25 p.p.; Single £33-35. 75 percent discount for children.
Vouchers accepted. **Credit cards:** Yes. **Open:** January to December
24. **Children:** All ages. **Pets:** Yes. **Smoking:** Nonsmoking rooms available. **Provision for handicapped:** Yes, 1 room. **Directions:** At the city
tourist office facing north, drive to first traffic light. Turn left onto
N22. Drive straight through toward Killarney, but after crossing river,
turn left just before Crow's Nest pub. Victoria Lodge is 10 meters
(almost 33 feet) on your right.

This four-star Irish Tourist Board-rated luxury guesthouse is situated in a mature, peaceful garden on the west side of Cork City. This
former monastery, newly renovated, offers great accommodations for
visiting the sights in Cork, just minutes away from the City Center
and convenient to Tennis Village. It offers guests color TV, semi-
orthopedic beds, lifts to each floor, direct-dial telephone, tea-making
facilities, and a secure car park—a modern lodging in all regards.
Breakfast is the full Irish Breakfast, and/or delicious menu items.
The warmth of welcome is unsurpassed. Golf clubs, museums, and
fishing facilities are not too far away. Frank tried his hand at catching
salmon on the Lee River, but the big ones got away.

The Lighthouse
Carmel Kelly-O'Gorman
The Rock
Kinsale, County Cork
Telephone: 021-772734; **FAX:** 021-774206
Bedrooms: 4, all with private baths.
Rates: £25 p.p.; £30 p.p. (private suite); Single £38; discount for children. Vouchers not accepted. **Credit cards:** VISA, MasterCard/Access, Eurocard. **Open:** All year. **Children:** Yes, 12 and older. **Pets:** No. **Smoking:** Restricted. **Provision for handicapped:** None. **Directions:** Take R607 to town. At the White House Hotel, bear left, follow the white line for 2 minutes (⅓ mile), and go straight through the crossroads behind the museum. Tap Tavern will be on the left. The road goes right; follow the white line past St. Moltose Church to the top of the hill. The Lighthouse is on the right.

This elegant bed and breakfast was built on the site of the old Kinsale Beacon. It has been completely renovated since the fire of 1993. Carmel, an interior decorator among other things, fashioned a B&B with a touch of class and refinement. Every room is appointed with antiques. One private suite has its own sitting room. The four-poster and canopy beds in the Georgian suite or the Empire room are beautiful. The Victorian dining room is in Regency style with old prints of London that provide a perfect match for the period decor. Breakfast features a choice of juices or raspberries in champagne, cereals (including honey muesli), yogurts, fancy teas, smoked salmon and scrambled eggs, Irish cheddar and other cheeses, black and white puddings, mushrooms, kippers with lemon butter, and so on. You will certainly have your fill of Irish delicacies. Carmel, with her professional approach to hospitality, will lead you to the best restaurants and make your visit to Kinsale a highlight of your trip to the Irish Republic. Her B&B is within easy reach of fishing, boating, 2 golf courses, and horseback riding.

Rivermount House
Claire O'Sullivan
Knocknabinny, Barrells Cross
Kinsale, County Cork
Telephone: 021-778033; **FAX:** 021-778225
Bedrooms: 6, all with private baths.
Rates: £17-20 p.p.; 20 percent discount for children. Vouchers accepted. **Credit cards:** None. **Open:** February 1 to December 1. **Children:** All ages. **Pets:** Yes. **Smoking:** Yes. **Provision for handicapped:** Ground-floor accommodations. **Directions:** Continue on R600 through Kinsale to the Old Head. Go over the bridge and turn right. Continue for 9/10 mile to the large crossroad. Turn right; Rivermount is 4th house on the right. It is almost 2½ miles from Kinsale on the road to Ballinspittle.

This large, lovely modern, country home situated on a four-acre lot in a quiet setting with spectacular views of the Brandon River has a great deal of charm and character. There are many amenities such as baby sitting, TVs, tea- and coffee-making facilities, telephones, radios, hairdryers, and private off-street parking. The bedrooms are pink with matching fabrics, the large lounge has warm red walls and green carpeting, and the bright and airy conservatory is yellow and green. A luxurious decor exists throughout the whole house and is obvious the minute you enter. The breakfast is varied from traditional to salmon or pancakes; the emphasis is on home produce. Nearby there is sailing (Kinsale is one of the largest recreational sailing centers in all of Ireland), fishing, beaches, and horseback riding. Also, Kinsale hosts a gourmet restaurant festival in the fall, but you will find good eating here any time of the year. There are many quaint and extraordinary restaurants where you find gourmet and country fare served in varied ambiences.

Walyunga
Myrtle Levis
Sandycove
Kinsale, County Cork
Telephone: 021-774126
Bedrooms: 5; 4 with private baths, 1 with shared.
Rates: £16 p.p. private bath; £14 p.p. shared bath; Single £18-22; 20 percent discount for children under 12. **Credit cards:** None. **Open:** February 1 to beginning of November. **Children:** Yes, 5 or older. **Pets:** No. **Smoking:** Restricted. **Provision for handicapped:** None. **Directions:** As you approach Sandycove, you will see Walyunga sign. Follow the sign. Walyunga is about 2 miles from Trident. Call if you need further directions.

This pleasant couple offers a modern country home with hanging plants and a feeling of openness to nature by a creative use of glass and skylights. There are grand views of the Atlantic Ocean with a lighthouse in the distance through large picture windows. A sliding glass door in front opens to a garden and meadow. Mr. Levis, an elementary-school teacher, knows the natural history of the region, and gives advice on genealogical quests. They had spent many years in Australia, thus the name Walyunga. All rooms are modern and spacious with fluffy quilts. One is a front corner room with a large bed and spacious bath that we took to be the "honeymoon suite." The pastel colors in the rooms with fine furniture and woodwork make this an attractive home. The sun was brilliant when we were there, and the delicious breakfast with brewed coffee and a view out the front was memorable. They offer a variety of cereals, porridge, fruit salad, yogurt, smoked salmon, and scrambled eggs in addition to an Irish Breakfast. Nearby are sandy beaches, fishing, and scenic coastal walks. The sailboats in the harbor, the restaurants, and the quaint seaport make Kinsale a special place.

Ballymakeigh House
Margaret Browne
Killeagh
Youghal, County Cork
Telephone: 024-95184; **FAX:** 024-95370
Bedrooms: 5, all with private baths.
Rates: £25-35 p.p.; Single £5 extra; 50 percent discount for children.
Vouchers not accepted. £20-22 dinner. **Credit cards:** All major ones.
Open: February to November. **Children:** All ages. **Pets:** Negotiable.
Smoking: Restricted. **Provision for handicapped:** None. **Directions:**
Go straight between "Old Thatch" (where there is a sign for Bally-
makeigh House) and the church in Killeagh when turning off the
N25. Their driveway is on the right about ½ mile.

This stately and refined 18th-century farmhouse, elegantly decorated by Mrs. Browne, is a showpiece for decor and colors. The
Brownes were the 1992 winners of the A.I.B./I.F.J. Agri-Tourism
National Award for Best Farmhouse B&B. In 1997 Mrs. Browne won
the A.A. Land Lady of the Year Award. There is a glassed-in conservatory for lounging and teas. The bedrooms are spacious with charming views of the meadows. They have extras like French soap,
facecloths, hairdryers, and suitcase racks. One room is done in cream
and rose with a flowered duvet and a large bathroom with a tub and
wood floor, another with blue and pink and a lovely blue and white
tiled bathroom. The dining room is done in green and red with an
antique piano. Fresh flowers abound. Gourmet cooking by your host
will delight your palate both at breakfast and at dinner. For breakfast
you get a choice of free-range eggs, porridge, fresh orange juice,
grapefruit, or apple juice. Kippers are offered too. Tennis courts are
on the grounds. They also have a game room and play area. Three golf
courses are nearby and the house is convenient to Midleton Heritage
Park, Fota, Trabolgan, Vee, Blarney, Cork Airport and Ferryport, Bal-
lymaloe, and sandy beaches.

ALSO RECOMMENDED

Blarney, *Emerald House,* Bridget Murphy, The Square. Telephone: 021-385148. Bedrooms: 4, all with private baths. Vouchers accepted. Period house nearest to castle entrance overlooking the town common. Walking distance to Blarney Woolen Mills, restaurants, and Blarney Park Hotel, where there is music, dancing, and swimming. Tea/coffee facilities. Color TVs in rooms.

Blarney, *St. Anthony's,* Mr. Pat O'Flynn, Sunset Place, Killeens. Common's Road, on N617. Telephone: 021-385151. Bedrooms: 6, 3 with private baths. 5 minutes to Cork City. Country home in scenic surroundings.

Blarney, *The White House,* Pat and Regina Coughlin, Blarney Town. Telephone: 021-385338. Bedrooms: 6, 4 with private baths. ½ mile from Blarney Center on the Mallow road.

Clonakilty, *Inchydoney Hotel,* Colette and Denis Murphy, managers, Inchydoney. Telephone: 023-33143. Bedrooms: 29, 23 with private baths. Family-owned and -operated hotel that has the feel of a country home B&B. Apartments also available. 2 beaches nearby, tennis, fishing, golf, and indoor and outdoor playgrounds. Recommended by Betty Ann and John Callanan of Hampton, N.H.

Glengarriff, *Cois Coille,* Rita Barry-Murphy. Telephone: 027-63202. Bedrooms: 5, 3 with private baths. Comfortable country home overlooking Glengarriff Harbor. Recommended by Angela Muckley, a founder of the Town and Country Homes Association.

Gougane Barra, *Gourgane Barra Hotel,* Christopher and Breda Lucey, Ballingeary. Telephone: 026-47069/47223; FAX: 026-47226. Bedrooms: 28, all with private baths. Lovely guesthouse on its own grounds tucked away in beautiful mountains of West Cork. Inland from Glengarriff overlooking Gougane Barra Lake, the source of the Lee River. Family-owned and -operated hotel. The favorite of Dan Callanan of Beverly Cove, Mass.

Kinsale, *Griffin's Hillside House,* Margaret Griffin, Camp-Hill, on the hill above Kinsale Town. Telephone: 021-772315. Bedrooms: 6, 3 with private baths. Open all year. Beautiful sea view.

Kinsale, *The Moorings Guesthouse,* Pat and Irene Jones, Scilly. Telephone: 021-772376. Bedrooms: 8 (luxury), all with private baths.

Breakfast served in elegant conservatory overlooking the estuary, forts, and yacht marina.

Kinsale, *The Old Presbytery,* Ken and Cathleen Buggy. Cork Street, Kinsale Town. Bedrooms: 6, 4 with private baths. Unusual B&B, an old Victorian house tastefully decorated with antiques both decorative and functional.

Skibbereen, *Glencar,* Josephine Griffin, Cork Road, in suburbs of Skibbereen on N71. Telephone: 028-21638. Bedrooms: 5, 3 with private baths. 2 single bedrooms. Spacious house overlooking open countryside.

County Donegal

County Donegal, way up in the northwest corner of Ireland, has a definite rugged character all its own. Settlers came here in 7000 B.C. It doesn't seem to suffer from being almost entirely bordered on the east by Northern Ireland. You could spend a week or two there and not see all the wonderful and varied sights. To the northwest, it is very mountainous, and the N56 takes you on a grand tour of the seacoast with its hundreds of inlets and wonderful fishing villages on the Atlantic Ocean. You'll find great rock formations and fine sandy beaches for swimming and surfing.

If you decide to travel up the eastern side of Lough Swilly to see the ancient ruins and castles of the spectacular Inishowen Peninsula, the R38 makes a circular tour. This area was settled by Normans in the 10th century.

Letterkenny seems to be the most central city for all these trips and it's a fun town to visit on its own. Tourist Information is on Derry Road and open June to September. The majestic St. Euman's Cathedral is especially pretty lit up at night. Visit the Donegal County Museum on High Road, and choose from a number of good pubs downtown almost any night in summer for singalongs and traditional Irish music. Two good restaurants are the Gleneany House and The Silver Tassie in Letterkenny. Golf, fishing, and swimming are very close at hand. From here it's only 30 minutes northwest to the unspoiled wildness of Glenveagh National Park, with its Castle and Gardens on 25,000 acres and beautiful, dramatic views of mountains, rivers, and vales. Letterkenny is a good home base for a trip around to the Antrim coast, with the peculiar, enormous, step-rock formation called the Giant's Causeway. It's a quick ride to the thriving, exciting town of Derry, too. Try the excellent DaVinci's Restaurant for atmosphere and great choices. On the way, through Carrigans, in eastern Donegal, you'll find charming country scenes and vistas, a photographer's dream.

To the south is the lovely Lough Eske and Donegal, a small town with charm, great for shopping and trying dinners in good hotels and restaurants. You'll find handcrafted woolen goods and Donegal tweeds for sale in the shops. Donegal Castle is a walk from the Diamond in the center of town. Ask where the good Irish music is playing in lounges and pubs. It's very popular there. Hyland Central Hotel has a good Sunday Buffet.

Travel out west of Donegal on the N15 to Killybegs, with its fishing fleet. When we were in County Wexford, clear across the country, we met a man who said he traveled every week to fish on his boat out of Killybegs, as the fishing is so good there. It's a pleasant drive north to the fishing villages of Portnoo, Ardara, and Glencolumbkille, with its Folk Park, all on the Atlantic Ocean.

Ballyshannon is the southern gateway to Donegal County. It has a musical Folk Festival every July or August. Visit Belleek with its delicate pottery, just a few miles away on the Fermanagh border and visit the neat beaches of Rossnowlagh, where you can surf or water-ski.

Cavangarden House
Agnes McCaffrey
Ballyshannon, County Donegal
Telephone: 072-51365
Bedrooms: 6, all with private baths.
Rates: £17 p.p.; Single £22; 50 percent discount for children. Vouchers accepted. £12 dinner on request. **Credit cards:** All major ones. **Open:** March 1 to November 1. **Children:** All ages. **Pets:** No. **Smoking:** Yes. **Provision for handicapped:** None. **Other features:** Plenty of parking. **Directions:** The house is 11 miles south of Donegal Town on the N15 on the right, or 3 miles north of Ballyshannon on the left.

We drove down a country lane with sheep and cows grazing on either side and came to a stately 1750 stucco manor house. Mrs. McCaffrey graciously served us tea in the classically decorated, high-ceilinged living room, by the marble fireplace. Antique gold-framed mirrors and pictures graced the walls and a conversation piece was a fancy lounge couch covered in caramel-colored velvet. The rooms were a surprise with oversized antique mahogany beds, comfy quilts, and handsome dark bureaus and tables. Walls all have large-floral-printed paper, Victorian style. The two rooms on the third floor are more modern and sunny with skylights. Pastoral scenes and bright green hills can be seen from each room. Cavangarden House reminded us of a grand old house we stayed at in Limoges, France. The castle-sized dining room has a very long, dark, wood table and carved-back chairs. In addition to the Irish Breakfast, Mrs. McCaffrey serves yogurt and fruit and features delicious homemade scones. Rossnowlagh Beach is 3 miles away with swimming and windsurfing and the house is quite near to Donegal Town.

Mount Royd
Josephine Martin
Carrigans (near Derry), County Donegal
Telephone: 074-40163
Bedrooms: 4, all with private baths.
Rates: £17 p.p.; Single £19; 50 percent discount for children under 12.
Vouchers accepted. £12 dinner; £6.50 high tea. **Credit cards:** None.
Open: All year, except Christmas Day. **Children:** Yes. **Pets:** Yes. **Smoking:** Restricted. **Provision for handicapped:** None. **Directions:** Carrigans has signs posted on the N13 and N14. From Derry City, take Letterkenny Road (A40) and stay on A40 to Carrigans. Mount Royd is on left. From Letterkenny, take the N13 until you see signs for Carrigans.

This elegant 1940s Georgian country home is one of our favorites because of the pastoral setting and the extraordinary care that Mrs. Martin has taken in decorating and furnishing her spacious home. It was a farmhouse and they still have sheep grazing in the meadows of their 12 acres. Your hostess greets you with tea and her special apricot or nut scones, and she shows you a video of the highlights of the region in the cozy living room in front of the fire. Recently she has won the Galtee Irish Breakfast Award and is now AAS elected (4Qs). The guest rooms are all large and very lovely with lots of ruffles in varying shades of pink, blue, or peach. Laura Ashley printed quilts grace the beds and each large bath has fancy colored soaps matching Mrs. Martin's theme. The pink room has a butterfly theme. One bedroom is pink and rose and has a fireplace. The breakfast is served in her handsome dining room with a trolley of apricots, grapefruit, and mandarin oranges, fresh fluffy scones, and home-baked currant bread in addition to a choice of omelet or fried eggs, bacon and sausage, or yogurt, cheese, and cereal. The Martins love to tell of Agatha Christie living and writing her mysteries in a big house just across the road. Derry is only 5 miles away with excellent restaurants like DaVinci's, to name one good one we favor. This is a good base for touring the Inishowen Peninsula, Londonderry, and the fascinating Giant's Causeway on the coast of Antrim. Also 5 miles away is the Cavanacor Historic House and Craft Center, the ancestral home of U.S. President James Polk. A historic fort, Grianan of Aileach, is nearby, too.

Ardeevin
Mary McGinty
Lough Eske, Barnesmore
Donegal Town, County Donegal
Telephone and **FAX:** 073-21790
Bedrooms: 5; 4 with private baths, 1 private not in room.
Rates: £18 p.p.; Single £21; 10 percent discount for children under 12.
Vouchers accepted. £13 dinner on request. **Credit cards:** None. **Open:**
March 31 to October 31. **Children:** All ages. **Pets:** No. **Smoking:** No.
Provision for handicapped: None. **Directions:** Going south from Let-
terkenny on the N15, 2 miles after Biddy O'Barnes' Pub on the right,
turn right. Follow the signs down the winding country road for about
1 mile. Out of Donegal Town, follow Derry Road (N15) for 3½ miles
until you come to a fork in the road. Turn left, follow the signs to
Lough Eske, then follow the *Ardeevin* sign the rest of the way.

Mary McGinty and her husband, a charming and hospitable couple, run the nicest B&B country home, which is newly renovated. The
bedrooms are pretty, with flowered duvets in pinks and blues and
handsome mahogany wood headboards. All rooms, including the dining room, have an exquisite view of Lough Eske. Tea- and coffee-making facilities are in each room. You are close to Donegal Town with its
restaurants and shops. Visit McGinty's knitting shop for some real bargains. But this place is a delight because of its beautiful rooms, the spacious dining room with lake views, and genuinely friendly hosts. The
buffet-style breakfast has a full array of delicious offerings like Kippers and seafood crepes, but we were thrilled with the pancakes and
syrup. Other offerings were fresh fruit, yogurt, cheese and scones, and
of course the Irish Breakfast. We enjoyed the Sunday special dinner
at Harvey's Point restaurant across the lake too! This is an ideal base
for horseback riding, fishing, hiking nearby, and golf, 8 miles away at
Rossnowlagh.

Bannagh House
Phyllis Melly
Fintra Road
Killybegs, County Donegal
Telephone: 073-31108
Bedrooms: 4, all with private baths.
Rates: £17 p.p.; Single £21; 10 percent discount for children. Vouchers not accepted. **Credit cards:** None. **Open:** Easter to October 31. **Children:** All ages. **Pets:** No. **Smoking:** Restricted. **Provision for handicapped:** Yes. **Directions:** From Killybegs town, go 300 m west on main Glean Cholm Cille Road—the house is on the left overlooking the harbor.

This lovely modern house, built up on a hill, has sliding glass doors and large windows for a great view of Killybegs Harbor and the fishing fleet. Phyllis's 4 rooms are all on one level and attractively decorated in soft colors. They all have tea- and coffee-making facilities, TVs, hairdryers, and electric blankets. We had a quick tour, because she was going out the door when we arrived. But she was gracious anyway and took time to show us through. The lounge has TV and turf fires, and both the lounge and the dining room have a wonderful water view. Her Irish Breakfast includes cereals, homemade hot scones and breads, jams, and treacle bread. Killybegs is a large fishing port so a visitor can go fishing or pleasure boating in the harbor. Donegal Town is only 29 km away and there are scenic walks in the area. Fintra Beach is only 1.6 km away. The B&B has a garage for bikes, and there is private parking.

Lismolin Country Home
Bernie Cahill
Fintra Road
Killybegs, County Donegal
Telephone: 073-31035 and 073-32310; **FAX:** 073-32310
Bedrooms: 5, all with private baths.
Rates: £16 p.p.; Single £21; 33½ percent discount for children.
Vouchers accepted. £13 dinner. **Credit cards:** VISA, MasterCard,
Access. **Open:** All year, except 3 days of Christmas. **Children:** All ages.
Pets: No. **Smoking:** Restricted. **Provision for handicapped:** Can take
wheelchairs. **Directions:** Go west through Killybegs town toward Glen-
columbkille; 1 km west of Killybegs, take the street on the left. The
B&B is the first house on the left; a single-level ranch with a tile roof.

The turf fire was burning during our visit, and Bernie's hospitality
was captivating. This lovely modern home is situated beside a verdant
forest and has a picturesque view of Cronard Mountain across the
road. All rooms are redecorated each year, but you will find trebles,
doubles, and singles—all kinds of accommodations—in pretty floral
patterns (dark blue and white or peach, or grey and pink) with baths
to match. There are electric blankets on all beds. All have TVs and
hairdryers. Being off the street, the house is quiet. The car park in
front makes it convenient for getting in and out for your day trips. The
spacious dining room has 5 separate tables with royal-blue tablecloths.
The red and violet hydrangea in the garden outside can be seen from
the sliding glass door in the fireplaced dining room. This is a pleasant place to have one of Bernie's delicious cooked breakfasts accom-
panied by porridge and homemade soda and brown breads, slathered
with her own black currant, gooseberry, or rhubarb jelly. Broiled fish
is also featured. Pleasure-boat and deep-sea-fishing trips can be
arranged. Try the Blue Haven Restaurant nearby for good, reason-
ably priced food.

Ardglas
Breid and Paddy Kelly
Lurgybrack, Sligo Road
Letterkenny, County Donegal
Telephone: 174-22516/25140
Bedrooms: 6, all with private baths, 1 extra bath in the hall.
Rates: £17 p.p. private bath; Single £21; 30 percent discount for children under 12. Vouchers accepted. **Credit cards:** None. **Open:** April 1 to Mid-October. **Children:** All ages. **Pets:** No. **Smoking:** Restricted. **Provision for handicapped:** Yes. **Directions:** From Letterkenny, take Derry Road to Dry Arch Roundabout to the N13 (Sligo Road). Go 1 mile—the house is on the left.

This beautiful house with many windows is high on a hill and some of the rooms look out onto grazing sheep and mountain views. The Kellys have dogs and cats. Breid is most gracious as a hostess. The modern living room is large with a TV, flagstone fireplace, and soft cocoa-colored chairs. All the rooms are very attractive and have matching duvets in flowered prints of quiet colors such as beiges, pinks, and browns. The upstairs rooms are larger. All of the rooms have TVs, hairdryers, and tea-making facilities. Breid has 4 family rooms. Her Irish Breakfast includes fresh fruit, yogurt, and cereal, boiled or poached eggs, or porridge. Paddy and his son both teach woodworking in secondary schools. It is an ideal place for visiting North Donegal, Derryveagh Mountains, and Northern Ireland's wonderful seacoast. It is close to golf, fishing, bowling, and horseback riding, and you'll find 3 cinemas as well as a leisure center in town.

Glencairn House
Maureen McCleary
Ramelton Road
Letterkenny, County Donegal
Telephone: 074-24393/25242
Bedrooms: 6; 5 with private baths, 1 private not in room.
Rates: £15-17 p.p.; Single £20; ⅓ discount for children under 12.
Vouchers accepted. **Credit cards:** All major ones. **Open:** All year,
except Christmas week. **Children:** All ages. **Pets:** No. **Smoking:**
Restricted to lounge. **Provision for handicapped:** Rooms on ground
floor. **Directions:** Coming into Letterkenny take Ramelton Road
(R245) to the right. As you climb the hill, Glencairn House is on your
right. Drop down into the large car park. This home is near Mount
Errigul Hotel.

This modern suburban home on a hillside is gorgeous. From the
etching on the front door, to the large gold and beige bathroom, to
the spacious room with a spectacular view of the whole valley—all is
beautiful! You may see the Swilly River valley from the side patio,
which has lounge chairs. The pink and green, beige and pale apricot,
and grey and pink in the bedrooms give them a soft and elegant look.
All headboards are covered in velvet. Rooms have tea- and coffee-making facilities and TV. The family room on the right is Frank's favorite.
It has a double and single bed, dressing table or desk, and large bath
in the back. The large lounge with a fireplace will be where you are
greeted with tea or coffee on your arrival. A full Irish Breakfast is
served with fruit, yogurt, cheese, cereal, and porridge in the large
dining room, which has separate tables and a view. This place is a great
bargain! Golf, bowling, and 3 cinemas are in the area. Ask for directions to good salmon fishing, too.

Hill Crest House
Larry and Margaret Maguire
Lurgybrack
Letterkenny, County Donegal
Telephone: 074-22300/25137
Bedrooms: 6; 5 with private baths, 1 private not in room.
Rates: £20 p.p. private bath ensuite; £15 p.p. unattached bath; Single
£20-25; 33 percent discount for children under 12. Vouchers
accepted. **Credit cards:** Yes, all but Diners. **Open:** All year, except 5
days at Christmas. **Children:** All ages. **Pets:** No. **Smoking:** Restricted.
Provision for handicapped: Yes, if they are with help. **Directions:** From
Letterkenny, take the N14 towards Derry; at Dry Arch Roundabout,
take the N13 (Sligo Road). The house is 1 km up the road on the
right, past the school.

This modern house with a car park sits on a hill, so some of the
rooms have a grand view of the town and river. The very cozy guest
lounge has a TV, VCR, and fireplace; you can peruse the many
brochures in a neat rack of all the nearby places to visit. The bedrooms are blue, pink, beige, and orange, all with TVs, orthopedic
beds, and electric blankets. The two upstairs rooms have terrific views.
Margaret and Larry were just unpacking their new delftware with wildflowers and matching napkins when we arrived. They served us tea,
scones, and tarts in their large kitchen, where we met three of their
five children. The dining room has lace tablecloths and Margaret
serves a routine full Irish Breakfast along with fruit, yogurt, and
choices of eggs. The Maguires conceived and published a brochure
that shows different tour routes to Glencolumbkille to the south, with
5,000 years of history, Inishowen Peninsula in northern Donegal;
Fanad and Rosguill circuits; and the Gaelacht Heritage trail including Glenveagh Castle and Gardens.

Town View B&B
May and Danny Herrity
Leck Road
Letterkenny, County Donegal
Telephone: 074-21570/25138
Bedrooms: 6, all with private baths.
Rates: £16 p.p.; Single £21; 25 percent discount children under 12.
Vouchers accepted. **Credit cards:** None. **Open:** All year. **Children:**
Yes, 5 or older. **Pets:** No. **Smoking:** Restricted. **Provision for handi-
capped:** Yes. **Directions:** From the center of town, take Main Street to
the foot of the hill to Dunnes Store, go left, cross over the bridge,
and stay left for ½ mile; follow the signs to the B&B.

A modern, white-stucco bungalow, this B&B has pleasantly comfortable rooms all decorated in pastel blues and geens. May is a great
hostess, serving you tea on arrival and leading you on a good tour
around the area. The view of the whole town from her sitting room is
spectacular by day or night. Beautiful lamps and antiques adorn the
house and the dining room is spacious with views also. Breakfast is a
gourmet delight with a buffet of lots of fruits, cereals, yogurts, and
cheeses in addition to her full cooked Irish Breakfast. She has won a
Galtee award for her good breakfasts. Danny and her son and daughter help with the work; Dan has a horse of his own in a little barn. A
large car park is available, and golf, ten-pin bowling, and a swimming
pool are open to visitors of Letterkenny town. They are close to the
famous Glenveagh Castle and Gardens, and Rathmullan Beach. One
night we drove to Derry for an excellent dinner.

Thalassa Country Home
Eva Friel
Narin
Portnoo, County Donegal
Telephone: 075-45151
Bedrooms: 4, all with private baths.
Rates: £17 p.p.; Single £18.50; 20 percent discount for chldren under 12. Vouchers accepted. £12.50 dinner; £8 high tea. **Credit cards:** None. **Open:** February to November. **Children:** All ages. **Pets:** No. **Smoking:** Restricted. **Provision for handicapped:** None. **Directions:** Take the N56 to Ardara, then R261 to Portnoo-Narin, about 6 km. Follow the sign for Portnoo. The house is on the coast road overlooking the ocean and golf course.

If ocean views are your choice, this modern country home will provide you with plenty of breathtaking scenery in this beautiful part of Donegal. Mrs. Friel keeps a nice bed and breakfast and comes highly recommended by other B&B owners. She serves a home-cooked Irish Breakfast with yogurt, fruit, and a choice of cereals. The house has bay windows in front for ocean views. A beautiful garden graces the front yard with folding chairs to lounge in during the off hours. The rooms are well decorated and furnished and there is a comfortable lounge with a TV. You will receive an especially warm welcome, and baby-sitting can be arranged while you play golf at the nearby 18-hole course or go out for a pint at the local pub. This quiet location has forest walks and trips to historic monuments. Visit gorgeous Gweebarra Bay, with a long stretch of sandy beaches, just a 10-minute walk away. The water is safe for bathing.

ALSO RECOMMENDED

Bruckless, *Bruckless House,* Clive and Joan Evans. Telephone: 073-37071; FAX: 073-37070. Bedrooms: 5, 2 with private baths. Clive breeds traditional Irish draft horses and Connemara ponies. Home handsomely decorated and appointed. On N56 towards Killybegs. Bruckless House on left in the village of Bruckless.

Donegal, *Eske View,* Mary and Keith Pearson, Lough Eske, Barnesmore. Telephone: 073-22087. Bedrooms: 3, 2 with private baths.

Donegal, *Woodlands,* Mrs. Bernie McGonigle, Coast Road, Doonan. Telephone: 073-21453. Bedrooms: 5, all with private baths. 1 km west of Donegal Town. Recommended by Brid and Walter Myles of Cavan Town.

Killybegs, *Glenlee House,* Mrs. Ellen O'Keeney, Fintra Road. Telephone: 073-31026. Bedrooms: 5, all with private baths. Very nice. Recommended by Mary McGinty of Lough Eske, Donegal.

Killybegs, *Lough Head House,* Mrs. Sadie McKeever, Donegal Road. Telephone: 073-31088. Bedrooms: 3, 2 with private baths. Vouchers accepted. Panoramic view of Killybegs Harbor. Smokefree home.

Rossnowlagh, *Ardeelen Manor,* Mrs. Fun Britton. Telephone: 072-51578. Bedrooms: 4. Recommended by Walter and Brid Myles of Cavan Town.

COUNTY DUBLIN

County Dublin

County Dublin is nearly the smallest county in Ireland, but by no means the least important. The capital city of Dublin dominates the area, taking up about one-fifth of the county. Besides the city center, suburban areas such as Clontarf, Drumcondra, Raheny, and Fairview to the north, and Ballsbridge, Donnybrook, Rathmines, and Sandymount to the south, are all considered part of Dublin City.

Dublin Center is a very exciting visit with all its history and culture. The best way to get a sense of it all is to ride a tour bus from O'Connell Street, with colorful commentary, all around, and see the museums, theaters, cathedrals, Trinity College with its famed *Book of Kells,* Saint Stephen's Green, the Liffey River with its "humpy" bridges, well-known Grafton Street (no traffic) for shopping and buskers playing sweet music, the National Gallery and Government buildings, and the Post Office, still with marks of the Easter Rebellion of 1916. For genealogical study, stop at the National Library on Kildare Street and the General Register Office of Births, Marriages, and Deaths at Joyce House, 8/10 Lombard St. East. You may get off at any stop and pick up where you left off in an hour or two and continue the tour.

Dublin City spawned and is very proud of its great writers such as James Joyce, Jonathan Swift, Samuel Beckett, Sean O'Casey, Brendan Behan, Kate O'Brien, Oscar Wilde, Mary Lavin, George Bernard Shaw, Brian Friel, Maeve Binchy, Christy Brown, and many others. Visit the James Joyce Cultural Centre at 35 North Great George's St. There is a whole walking tour you may take of the spots visited by Leopold Bloom, the hero of *Ulysses.* Dublin even celebrates "Bloomsday" on June 16 each year.

Be sure to visit the Dublin Zoo; Phoenix Park; the Bewleys Cafe on Grafton Street, with its delicious fresh coffee and food and its delightful James Joyce Room; and many of the old and charming pubs, some with traditional music. Scan the papers for current plays at the Abbey, the Peacock, and the Gate theaters. We found them very enjoyable. The original Abbey Theatre was started by William Yeats and Lady Gregory.

Outlying districts have beautiful old Dublin homes; go east to

71

Howth on a point of land that has the lighthouse called "The Eye of Ireland," and visit the restaurants and the Abbey Tavern in Howth, where a show of traditional Irish music is played nightly. In Clontarf, there is St. Anne's Rose Garden to visit and an excellent restaurant, The Yacht, on Clontarf Road, with super choices and good prices, especially at noon. Of course, Dublin Airport is just 20 minutes from Clontarf, Drumcondra, or Raheny. North and near the airport is the town of Malahide, with its smart castle and grounds and lovely old buildings downtown. To the south Ballsbridge flaunts the R.D.S. Arena with its famous horse shows and other events, and the Jury's Hotel with their nightly cabaret show, which is an extravaganza. Sandymount and Merrion have great beaches. Farther south is Bray Head, a wonderful place to climb, with ocean views, and the lovely seaport of Dún Laoghaire with its beaches and ferries to Holyhead, England. Dún Laoghaire also has the famed Joyce Tower to visit.

The DART, a very efficient electrical railway system, operates to outlying areas as far as Howth to the north and Dún Laoghaire to the south. It begins at 6:30 A.M. and ends at 11:30 P.M. There is very extensive bus service to all areas. The Tourist Information Office (Tel. 01-747733) at 14 Upper O'Connell Street is open weekdays 9-5:30 and Saturdays 9-1. The Irish Tourist Board (Tel. 01-765872), at Baggot Street Bridge, is open weekdays only, 9-6.

PLACES OF GENERAL PUBLIC INTEREST

1. Writer's Museum	6. Trinity College	11. Dublin Castle
2. General Post Office	7. National Museum	12. St. Patrick's Cathedral
3. Abbey Theatre	8. National Library	13. Four Courts of Justice
4. Central Bus Station	9. Pearse Station	14. Parnell Square
5. Tara St. Station	10. St. Stephen's Green	15. Merrion Square

Aisling House
Frances and Robert English
19/20 St. Lawrence Road
Clontarf, Dublin 3, County Dublin
Telephone: 01-8339097; **FAX:** 01-8338400
Bedrooms: 6, all with private baths.
Rates: £22.50-25 p.p. private bath; Single £30-40; Vouchers not accepted. **Credit cards:** None. **Open:** All year, except Christmas week. **Children:** All ages. **Pets:** No. **Smoking:** Restricted to the lounge. **Provision for handicapped:** None. **Directions:** From Dublin, stay left of the Liffey River, go left before the Custom House and left after the bus station to Amiens Street, follow to North Strand to Fairview to Clontarf Road, and take a left at the Methodist Church onto St. Lawrence Road. Aisling House is on the left.

The Aisling House is two elegant Victorian houses combined and fronted by a lovely rose garden, with a fruit tree orchard and children's area to the rear. The location gives it easy access to the airport, ferry, and city center, and other amenities. It is beautifully restored with some very large bedrooms to accommodate families. Bedrooms vary in style from old Victorian floral to fresh, modern pastel pinks, cream and greens, and luxurious throw quilts on each bed. Each rooms has a remote control TV. In the dining room, each breakfast table has a different pottery milk jug, preserve bowl, and white and brown sugar bowls. Irish pottery by Stephen Pierce, Stonewall Jackson, and Nichalas Moss are on display here, and two stunning still-life oil paintings adorn the walls. Frances and Robert want guests to enjoy the fine decor and furnishings, but yet feel at home and relaxed as well. Breakfast consists of homemade compote of fruit, homemade muesli, scones, and breads as well as toast, all of which complement a typical cooked Irish Breakfast. Guests may serve themselves with fruit juice, whole grapefruit segments, and fresh fruits with an assortment of cereals on the side buffet before the main course.

Clonliffe Bed and Breakfast
Larry and Mary Weathermon
94 Clonliffe Road
Drumcondra, Dublin 3, County Dublin
Telephone: 01-837-9656; **FAX:** 01-837-9656; **Mobile:** 0882782-879
Bedrooms: 4; 2 with private baths, 2 with shared.
Rates: £18 p.p. private bath; £16 p.p. shared bath. £10 discount for children. **Credit cards:** VISA and Western. **Open:** All year. **Children:** All ages. **Pets:** Yes. **Smoking:** Yes. **Provision for handicapped:** None. **Directions:** From airport toward city, turn left at Guiness Welcome to Dublin sign. Go over railway bridge. House is on left, halfway down Cloniffe Road—an off license (liquor store) is across the street.

This attractive 1940s country-style town house is only 15 minutes from the airport and 5 minutes from the city center by car or by bus. The Weathermons will give you care and attention, and they will suggest the best ways to enjoy Dublin. Besides the Irish Breakfast, Mary will serve you vegan or vegetarian breakfasts including organic yogurt and fruit. The rooms are simple and tastefully decorated with bright and cheerful colors of peach and yellow. All rooms offer tea- and coffee-making facilities and hairdryers. You will notice fresh flowers and lovely polished wood floors in the common areas. There is a beach 5 minutes away; and tennis, golf, and bowling are only a 10-minute drive. The exciting city of Dublin—with its historic castles, structures, shopping, and wonderful theatrical productions—is only minutes away.

Torc House
Eileen Kelly
17 Seacourt, St. Gabriels Road
Clontarf, Dublin 3, County Dublin
Telephone: 01-8332547
Bedrooms: 3; 2 with private baths, 1 with shared.
Rates: £20 p.p. private bath; £18 p.p. shared bath; Single £28. Vouchers not accepted. **Credit cards:** None. **Open:** March to November.
Children: Yes, 12 or older. **Pets:** No. **Smoking:** Restricted to lounge.
Provision for handicapped: None. **Directions:** From Dublin, go left on Amiens Street to North Strand and Clontarf Road to Seafield and go left. The first right is St. Gabriels Road, opposite the church.

We have stayed here a number of times and Eileen is a wonderful hostess, always helpful with a cup of tea at the ready in the comfortable lounge with a TV. Her Pomeranian and a new Maltese named Gypsy follow her everywhere. Her interior-decoration skills show in all her pretty rooms and baths; one room is newly and exotically decorated in claret red and gold with cream rolled pillows; one has butterscotch flowered duvets with matching print wallpaper; her third room is lovely pink, green, and rose. She uses dried bouquets of flowers, and embroidery and lace on her towels. Besides her regular Irish Breakfast, she offers special food for people on low-fat diets, yogurt, lots of fruit and cereal, and sometimes porridge or French toast. The dining room looks out onto a garden terrace and is set with elegant fine china. They can park five cars safely off the street. Eileen has a great grasp of Dublin entertainment and will help with your itinerary. Walk to the beautiful St. Ann's Rose Garden, where there is tennis, or to the Dollymount Restaurant. You'll be 10 minutes from Howth and the beach, 20 minutes from the airport, and a walk to a bus for Dublin and all of its great culture and history.

The Villa
Marie McMahon
150 Howth Road
Clontarf, Dublin 3, County Dublin
Telephone: 01-833-2377
Bedrooms: 5; 4 with private baths, 1 with shared.
Rates: £18-20 p.p. all rooms; Single £20; Single in double room £28; 20 percent discount for children. Vouchers not accepted. **Credit cards:** None. **Open:** All year, except Christmas Day and St. Stephen's Day. **Children:** Yes. **Pets:** No. **Smoking:** Restricted to porch. **Provision for handicapped:** None. **Directions:** From Dublin Airport, take the Motorway (M1). Turn left at Red Church onto Collins Street. Continue through the residential area to the end and turn right on Howth Road. The Villa is the 8th house on right.

This delightful Tudor home is a period piece that shows a refined Edwardian decor with flocked burgundy wallpaper in the hallway, a 17th-century antique clock, beautiful prints and paintings, a crystal chandelier, and many other antiques. The atmosphere is comfortably luxurious but not overbearing. The solarium outside the lounge is perfect for letter writing and reading. The dining room looks out on the front garden and lawn. The bedrooms are rose and pink with floral decorations. All are neat as a pin. Even the single room is quite large. The bus stops at the Beachcomber across the street. The Hollybrook Hotel has become our favorite for the pub lunch with carvery; it is super! The Villa is operated by two very welcoming sisters who make you feel comfortable from the start. Their breakfast is full Irish or vegetarian if required. The brewed coffee is a hit with American visitors. In the afternoon, guests can sit in the rear garden and be surrounded by roses, other flowers, and songbirds at the feeder.

Willowbrook
Mary Mooney
14 Strandville Avenue East
Clontarf
Dublin 3, County Dublin
Telephone: 01-8333115
Bedrooms: 3, all with private baths.
Rates: £25 p.p.; Single £30; no discount for children. Vouchers not accepted. **Credit cards:** None. **Open:** December 31 to December 20. **Children:** No. **Pets:** No. **Smoking:** No. **Provision for handicapped:** None. **Directions:** From Dublin Airport, take the Motorway (M1) toward the city. After the red brick church on left, turn left at the next set of lights onto Collins Avenue. Then turn right onto Howth Road. At end of Howth Road, turn left onto Clontarf Road. Take the first left onto Strandville Avenue East.

This large brick house was built by a builder for himself, so it has beautiful cornices in each room and solid mahogany doors and windows. The bedrooms are spacious and have cream walls with very fresh pink, turquoise, and green curtains and bed covers. All rooms have orthopedic mattresses and electric blankets, coffee- and tea-making facilities and safes. Mary provides fresh fruit and flowers each day. She offers a traditional Irish Breakfast and a varied menu. The beautiful dining room has cream walls, royal blue carpeting, a Waterford crystal chandelier, and antique furniture. This house is close to Dublin City and closer to Howth with its lighthouse, walks, and great restaurants.

Calderwood House
Barry and Mary Memery
2 Calderwood Avenue
Drumcondra, Dublin 9, County Dublin
Telephone: 01-8379568; **FAX:** 01-8379568
Bedrooms: 4; 3 with private baths; 1 with shared.
Rates: £19 p.p. private bath; £17 p.p. shared bath; Single £5 extra; 50 percent discount for children 2-12 years; babies free. Vouchers not accepted. **Credit cards:** Yes. **Open:** January 10 to December 20. **Children:** All ages. **Pets:** No. **Smoking:** Restricted. **Provision for handicapped:** Yes. **Directions:** From the airport, take the N1 to the red brick church (Whitehall). Go to the fourth set of lights, turn left onto Griffith Avenue, then take your second left. The first 2-story building on the right is Calderwood House.

This tall brick building is 15 minutes from the airport or city center. Mary and Barry are very congenial and will help you plan tours through Dublin. Their rooms are all different, neat, and attractive; 3 are on the ground floor and 1 is upstairs. The en-suite one downstairs is all pale pinks and has a garden view. The upstairs room has a high ceiling with a lovely stained-glass window facing west, left over from when the house was a convent. The living and dining rooms have handsome original pine floors. They are proud of their freshly brewed coffee served at the Irish Breakfast with a choice of fruit and yogurt. In the pretty town-house area near Griffith Avenue, the house is close to many colleges and institutions. It is 10 minutes to the city by bus, and beaches, golf, and tennis are within 15 minutes' drive.

Parknasilla
Teresa Ryan
15 Iona Drive
Drumcondra, Dublin 9, County Dublin
Telephone: 01-8305724
Bedrooms: 4; 2 with private baths, 2 with shared.
Rates: £19 p.p. private bath; £17 p.p. shared bath; Single £20; 20 percent discount for children under 12. **Credit cards:** None. **Open:** All year, except December 21 to January 31. **Children:** All ages. **Pets:** Only guide dogs. **Smoking:** No. **Provision for handicapped:** None. **Directions:** Drive north from city center for 1.5 km to Drumcondra Road and go left at St. Alphonsus Road. The third right after the church is Iona Drive.

A beautiful Edwardian red brick home in a residential area close in to Dublin, this is an "Old Dublin" style house built in 1908. The dining room has a rich red marble fireplace and there is colored glass inside and outside of this elegant home. The rooms are pretty, spacious, and have high ceilings. Teresa Ryan is pleasant and very helpful to travelers. Her full Irish Breakfast is augmented with yogurt and fruit and a continental breakfast. They are near the Botanical Gardens, five minutes from the B&I Ferry, 15 minutes from the airport or downtown, and near buses. Book ahead as they are often full.

Ashbrook House
Mrs. Eve Mitchell
River Road
Ashtown, Castleknock
Dublin 15, County Dublin
Telephone: 01-8385660; **FAX:** 01-8386867
Bedrooms: 6, all with private baths.
Rates: £25-30 p.p.; Single £35; discounts for children. Vouchers not accepted. **Credit cards:** All except American Express. **Children:** All ages. **Pets:** No. **Smoking:** In lounge only. **Provision for handicapped:** None. **Directions:** Take the M50 motorway from the Dublin Airport. Exit at the N3 turnoff for Blanchardstown/Castleknock. Turn left at the roundabout, and onto another roundabout. Go stright on, until the next roundabout, where there is a pub on the left called the Halfway House Pub. Tun left at the pub, and go over a railway crossing to a crossroads. Turn left and Ashbrook House is the second gate on the left.

This attractive, large 1897 Georgian home is just 10 minutes from the airport and ten minutes from Dublin center. The bedrooms are all rather large with large baths, and one room has a marble fireplace. Eve has used salmon pink, blues, blue and yellow, and pink and white color schemes in her rooms. Some furniture is pine and one new room has knotty pine in tea, orange, and green colors. Another room is decorated in cranberry and white. All rooms look out onto handsome gardens and the countryside. Eve serves a buffet breakfast of cereals, fruit, juices, poached or boiled eggs, bacon, mushrooms, and tomatoes. There is a grass tennis court on the premises and golf courses and horseback riding areas are available. A good place to eat is the Halfway House Pub, which is fairly close.

Annesgrove
Anne D'Alton
28 Rosmeen Gardens
Dún Laoghaire, County Dublin
Telephone: 01-280-9801
Bedrooms: 4; 2 with private baths, 2 with shared.
Rates: £20 p.p. private bath; £18 p.p. shared bath; Single £25-35; 25 percent discount for children under 12. Vouchers not accepted. **Credit cards:** None. **Open:** Mid-January to Christmas. **Children:** Yes, ages 4 and up. **Pets:** No. **Smoking:** Restricted. **Provision for handicapped:** None. **Directions:** From town center, take Georges Street south and the first right after the stoplight is Rosmeen Gardens, opposite People's Park. The house is number 28, a few houses up on the left.

This attractive brick and stucco house was built in 1932. Your hostess, Anne D'Alton, exudes a pleasant, professional charm and is always close at hand to look after special requests. The rooms are neat and peaceful, tastefully decorated in greens and beiges with wall trims, duvets, and curtains that match. Mrs. D'Alton has graced her walls with her husband's delicate watercolor landscapes, and they certainly add a lot to the rooms. All rooms have sinks and plenty of heat and hot water. The sitting room has a TV and is quite cozy. The dining room, where you'll be served an Irish Breakfast and a choice of fruit or yogurt or porridge, cereal, and juice, looks out onto delightfully landscaped gardens a few steps down on a lower level. If you must leave before breakfast, Mrs. D'Alton offers a special rate. They are very close to People's Park, the waterfront and ferry terminal, buses, and the DART into Dublin. Visit the many fine restaurants in town, swim at Sandy Cove Beach, and play golf or tennis very nearby. The D'Altons will tell you where. And the DART ride into Dublin is only 20 minutes. Dún Laoghaire is an ideal location to start or finish a holiday in the Irish Republic.

Innisfree
Mrs. Maura Gorby
31 Northumberland Ave.
Dún Laoghaire, County Dublin
Telephone: 01-280-3093/280-5598
Bedrooms: 6; 4 with private baths, 2 with shared.
Rates: £18.50 p.p. private bath; £16 p.p. shared bath; Single £22-27; 25 percent discount for children. Vouchers not accepted. **Credit cards:** VISA, MasterCard. **Open:** All year. **Children:** All ages. **Pets:** No. **Smoking:** Yes. **Provision for handicapped:** None. **Directions:** From town center, go along Georges Street to the large Dunnes Store. Northumberland Avenue is just before the store and Innisfree is several houses up on the left.

This 1890s Victorian house is handsomely decorated in rich colors. Enter through the metal gate into a flagstoned yard and a pretty fan-windowed door greets you on this street of brightly colored doors. The welcoming hallway has velvety red flocked wallpaper and all the rooms have high ceilings giving a spacious feeling. All the bedrooms are very trim, handsomely decorated, and have fireplaces (used as decoration). Your breakfast will include fried tomatoes, juice, fruit, cereal, and yogurt and will be served in the dining room on the lower level with separate tables. The living room with a fireplace has Old-World, Edwardian elegance. The B&B is located near the pier, the ferry terminal, and within walking distance to downtown and the DART. Besides the beach, golf, and tennis, the rugby stadium on Lansdowne Road and Killiney Castle are only minutes north. The James Joyce Tower to the south makes a good visit, too.

Park View House
Helen Callanan
1 Rosmeen Gardens
Dún Laoghaire, County Dublin
Telephone: 01-280-6083
Bedrooms: 4; 2 with private baths, 2 with shared.
Rates: £20 p.p. private bath; £18 shared bath; Single £25-30; 25 percent discount for children under 12. Vouchers not accepted. **Credit cards:** None. **Open:** All year, except Christmas. **Children:** All ages. **Pets:** No. **Smoking:** Restricted. **Provision for handicapped:** None. **Directions:** From town center, go south on Georges Street. Rosmeen Gardens is 2 streets after the bus depot on the right, and Park View House is the first house on the right.

This 1890s red brick Victorian is right across the street from a large park with lovely gardens, and all the rooms have a view of the harbor. You may walk to the center of this charming village, to the port where ferries arrive from Holyhead and Liverpool, England. The ferry terminal is only 3 blocks from the house. Mrs. Callanan is entertaining and helpful. Her pale-green living room, with a fireplace and attractive antiques, is elegant. You may want to choose the cool, light-green rooms with gorgeous duvets or a large luscious raspberry room with a bay view. The full Irish Breakfast will be served in the pretty dining room with lots of glass windows for a view of Mrs. Callanan's prize rose garden to the back and side. Breakfast options include choice of eggs, fresh fish or smoked salmon some days, and yogurt and fresh fruit. Frank enjoyed the smoked salmon with scrambled eggs. Sandy Cove Beach is 15 minutes away, and tennis and golf, walks in the People's Park, and many good restaurants are right in town. The DART gets you to the center of Dublin in only 30 minutes.

Liscara
Jane Kiernan
Malahide Road
Kinsealy, County Dublin
Telephone: 01-848375; **FAX:** 01-8483751
Bedrooms: 6, all with private baths.
Rates: £17-19 p.p.; Single £25; 25 percent discount for children.
Credit cards: None. **Open:** February 1 to November 30. **Children:** All
ages. **Pets:** No. **Smoking:** No. **Provision for handicapped:** Yes. **Directions:** Drive to Fairview, turn right on Malahide Road at the end of
the park. Go 4 miles. Liscara is 4th house on the right, after Saint
Doulough's Church.

This brand-new, red brick manor house is a treat. On one acre,
there are cabbage fields and a nursery to the back of it. Jane Kiernan
is very attentive. Her husband is newly retired. The rooms are all large
and elegant; one is dark lavender, white, and pink; one double has a
spectacular view of fields and way out to the water and Howth.
Another room is robin's-egg blue. There is a room on the first floor
with wide bathroom access for the handicapped. The handsome dining room has 3 tables, a flowered white wall, and a teal rug. In addition
to her standard full Irish Breakfast, Jane serves fresh fruit and yogurt
and cheese or kippered herrings. There is baby-sitting available here
by their daughter. They are close to golf courses in Malahide and
Portmarnock, and fishing, boating, and bowling are also easily accessible. There is a 10 cinemas nearby and they are only 6 minutes to
the airport. Charming Malahide Castle and town are 2 minutes away.

Pebble Mill B&B
Monica Fitzsimons
Off Malahide Road
Kinsealy, County Dublin
Telephone: 01-846-1792
Bedrooms: 4, all with private baths.
Rates: £20 p.p.; Single £28; 50 percent discount for children. Vouchers not accepted. **Credit cards:** None. **Open:** All year except Christmas. **Children:** All ages. **Pets:** No. **Smoking:** No. **Provision for handicapped:** None. **Directions:** From the airport, take the N1 to the first roundabout, go all around, head back, and take the first left at Coachman's Inn. Go over a humpy bridge and take the first left marked *Kinsealy* (1 mile). Go right on Malahide Road; take the first left at the pet shop; the sign is on the right.

This stately neo-Georgian house sits on 4 acres in a farm area. The long driveway winds up with flower baskets hanging from posts on either side. The family ponies are in a corral next to the house. The decor in the large living room with TV is modern and creative. It has a white marble fireplace, very comfortable chairs, a carved horse, and a green rug. Monica, very kind and personable, puts you at ease from the start. All the rooms are large and well lighted with big windows and views of gardens and have TVs and hairdryers. One room has rainbow colors, one has rosebud designs, and there is 1 extra bath with a tub. The dining room is red and white with a sliding glass door to the outside. Along with her full Irish Breakfast you may have fruit or yogurt. The beach is 5 minutes away, and horseback riding, tennis, and golf are 10 minutes away, as well as Malahide Castle and town. It is only 6 minutes from the airport.

Mantua Guest House Bed and Breakfast
Sue Clarke
Seatown Road
Swords, County Dublin
Telephone: 01-840-1568
Bedrooms: 3, all with private baths.
Rates: £25 p.p.; 25 percent discount for children 12 and under. Vouchers not accepted. **Credit cards:** None. **Open:** February 1 to the end of October. **Children:** All ages. **Pets:** No. **Smoking:** No. **Provision for handicapped:** None. **Directions:** From the airport, take the N1 to the sixth roundabout, drive all the way around to head north again. Take the left at Seatown Road, where you'll see a bed and breakfast shamrock sign. Go 300 yards, and the Mantua Guest House is the first house on your right.

This charming home, a large dormered bungalow surrounded by lovely flower gardens, is lovingly cared for by Sue Clarke, and you will be treated well too. The rooms are nicely decorated in white, pink, or peach with flowered duvets. All rooms have TVs and tea- and coffee-making facilities, as well as windows looking out onto the gardens. The sitting room/dining room combination is beautifully decorated in greens and browns. It is a comfortable area for reading by the fire. Sue serves a traditional Irish Breakfast along with cereal, yogurt, and fruit. There are tennis courts on the property also. The Mantua Guest House is very close to the airport and is five minutes from the sea, golf courses, and horse stables.

ALSO RECOMMENDED

Donnybrook, *Bective House,* Deidre and Sheila Farrell, 2 Eglinton Terr. (off Donnybrook Road). Telephone: 01-269-2983. Bedrooms: 6, 5 with private baths. Nice home close to city center. Street is a little drab outside, but inside the young ladies maintain a very pretty bed and breakfast, recently redecorated. R.D.S. nearby, and Point Theater.

Donnybrook, *Hazelhurst,* Joan Donnellan, 166 Stillorgan Rd. Telephone: 01-283-8509. Bedrooms: 5, all with private baths. Modern town house right on the N11 across from University College Dublin. Extra large living room with fireplace for reading and writing. Major credit cards accepted. Accessible to city center and Dún Laoghaire ferry.

Dublin, *The Georgian House Guesthouse,* Annette O'Sullivan, 20 Lower Baggot St. Telephone: 01-8618832; FAX: 01-8618834. Bedrooms: 26, all with private baths. Discounts for children. Credit cards accepted. Lunch and dinner available. Restored Georgian town house located near St. Stephen's Green. Off-street parking. Recommended by Jean and Richard Higgins, Seattle, Wash.

Dún Laoghaire, *Duncree,* Mrs. C. O'Sullivan, 16 Northumberland. Telephone: 01-280-6118. Bedrooms: 4, all shared bath but with sink and mirror in rooms. Modest home but very nice hostess, within walking distance of shops and restaurants.

Lusk, *Carriage House,* Curtin Family. Telephone: 01-843-8857; FAX: 01-843-8933. Bedrooms: 5, all with private baths. "Purpose-built" house, which means it was built to be a B&B. Lots of amenities. In a town north of Dublin, 10 minutes to airport.

Malahide, *Lynfar,* Mrs. Margaret Farrelly, Kinsealy Lane. Telephone: 01-846-3897. Bedrooms: 5, 1 with private bath. Vouchers accepted. Close to Dublin Airport, beside Malahide Castle, 2 km to Malahide, home set in private grounds.

COUNTY GALWAY

County Galway

County Galway is one of the largest counties in Ireland and Galway City is known as the capital of the west of Ireland. This county has a ruggedness of terrain that differs from the soft greens of the south. Galway, with its rivers, mountains, bays, lakes, and seacoast, is very photogenic. In north Galway, have a look at the peaceful Killary Harbor, which separates Mayo and Galway. The fields of green sweeping down to blue water and gentle hills beyond are a sight to behold. Between tiny Leenane on the border and Letterfrack, visit the Kylemore Abbey. Although Letterfrack seems to be in the boondocks, there is a lovely woolen craft shop there with a tearoom with sandwiches and scones. Stay along the N59 to reach the stunning town of Clifden, called the capital of Connemara, sitting high on a hill. It has marvelous views of bays and high mountains, such as the Twelve Bens, which change colors with the light and the season.

Clifden has joys of its own—pretty B&Bs with views, excellent restaurants, and traditional Irish music right into October. We tried Mitchell's Restaurant and D'Arcy Inn; both were quite good. It's fun to shop and browse through the art galleries, too. When you tear yourself away from the specialness of Clifden, drive around along the coast and visit the pretty fishing towns of Roundstone and Cashel. For a shorter drive, go down the N59 through rough and rocky Connemara country (look for ponies and donkeys grazing) to Oughterard. This pretty town is right on Lough Corrib, which reportedly has the best fishing in Ireland.

Salthill and Galway Town are tied together and are noted for their beaches, called strands, and boardwalks. Salthill has the very large Leisureland Amusement Park, with a swimming pool and rides, and an 18-hole golf course. It's a refreshing walk along the beach just outside of Galway. Look for the Galway hookers, special fishing boats with very rounded sides and sails.

Galway City is old, with one-way streets and many, many shops and eating places. There are art galleries and two theaters, the An Tarbhdhearc on Middle Street and the Druid on Chapel Lane. Catch an

Irish music session any evening in summer at one of the many pubs. At the end of July or the beginning of August, the famous Galway Races run for 6 days with much music and festivities. Book way ahead, for the Irish fill the rooms for this event. Another event you might enjoy is the Oyster Festival the third or fourth weekend in September.

We spent some time in Spiddal, west of Galway, where a lot of Gaelic is spoken in the pubs, the accents are strong and melodious, and the spontaneous fiddling and singing is good. From Galway City, the N6 takes you straight across the mid-section of the country to Dublin. Visit the starkly beautiful Aran Islands at the opening of Galway Bay. It's a happy trip back in time.

South of Galway you'll find the sweet town of Kilcolgan, with its fishing rivers, and a bit farther there is the important, pretty, small town of Kinvara. This town has farms and horseback riding, Dunguaire Castle with a feast and costumes, and a little port with pastel buildings looking out on fishing boats sitting at the docks. We couldn't resist painting some of these scenes. Eat at Partners Restaurant: good food, good prices.

From Galway City, the N6 takes you straight across the midsection of the country to the N4 and on to Dublin. The town of Athenry, just to the east of Galway City, is noted in the song, "Fields of Athenry," an Irish favorite. Visit the castle there. In October, the largest Horse and Cattle Fair in Europe (called the Great October Fair) is held farther on at Ballinasloe out on the eastern border of the county.

Beach View House
Bridie Conneely
Oatquarter, Kilronan
Aran Islands (Inis Mór), County Galway
Telephone: 099-61141;
During the winter, in the U.S.A.: 1-617-393-4844
Bedrooms: 6; 3 with private baths, 3 with shared.
Rates: £15 p.p.; Single £19; 25 percent discount for children under 12.
Vouchers accepted. **Credit cards:** None. **Open:** May to September.
Children: All ages. **Pets:** Yes. **Smoking:** Yes. **Provision for handicapped:**
No. **Directions:** Take a ferry to Inis Mór from Galway or Rossaveel;
the bus to Rossaveel is provided with the ferry ticket. From the port on
the island, take a bus, pony trap, bike, or walk 6 km to the B&B.

Beach View is a large, family-run home with a sitting area in the
front yard. It is situated in a tranquil spot in the center of the island.
Bridie Conneely is charming and friendly. The 6 bedrooms are neat
and delightfully furnished in pleasing colors. Bridie includes scones
with her full Irish Breakfast. Recreational features in the area are
horseback riding, fishing, cycling, and swimming just two miles away
on the safe, sandy beach. The house is within walking distance to
famous Fort Dun Aengus and convenient to a restaurant and pub. Inis
Mór, "The Big Island," has the only harbor suitable for steamer dock-
ing. You may take a jaunting car ride around the island to see ring
forts or Dun Aengus perched on a 300-foot cliff above the sea. Bikes
are for rent, too. You may take ferries to other fascinating unique Aran
Islands during your stay. Gaelic is the everyday language, but polite
islanders will speak English.

Mallmore Country House
Kathleen Hardman
Ballyconneely Road
Clifden, County Galway
Telephone: 095-21460
Bedrooms: 6, all with private baths, plus separate full bath with tub.
Rates: £18.50 p.p.; 20 percent discount for children under 12. Vouchers accepted. **Credit cards:** None. **Open:** March 1 to November 1. **Children:** All ages. **Pets:** No. **Smoking:** Restricted. **Provision for handicapped:** 4 steps in front, but after that all on 1 floor. **Directions:** Outside Clifden 1 mile on Ballyconneely Road, look for Mallmore House sign on the right. Turn right at Connemara Pottery. Go up a narrow country road to their gate.

This is a beautiful 1790s manor house that had been built by a John Darcy, lord of this region. It reminds you of a French country home because of its rich flocked walls, arched doorways, and pretty hall lights. It has been completely renovated by the Hardmans. The dining room is luxurious with red wallpaper, antique vases and side tables, 6 to 8 separate meal tables covered with linens, ballooned curtains at all windows with shutters, and a fireplace. Award-winning breakfasts include pancakes, omelets, and smoked salmon. The spacious bedrooms are also handsomely decorated with armoires and velvet boudoir chairs, and some have bowed windows viewing the cheery garden and the scenic harbor beyond. Our room was more of a suite, with two antique chairs in the bowed window where we enjoyed reading and even watercolor painting. Rooms are individually decorated in soft pastels. The sitting room with a fire is ideal for curling up with a good book. The Hardmans are genuinely nice. They take special care of their guests and run the inn with a steady, gentle touch.

Castle View
Anne and Martin Kerins
Weir Road
Kilcolgan, County Galway
Telephone: 091-796172
Bedrooms: 4, all with private baths.
Rates: £16.50 p.p.; Single £21; ⅓ discount for children under 12.
Vouchers accepted. **Credit cards:** None. **Open:** All year. **Children:** All ages. **Pets:** Yes. **Smoking:** Restricted to lounge. **Provision for handicapped:** Yes, rooms on first floor. **Directions:** In the Village of Kilcolgan, note the sign for Castle View and Moran's Seafood. Go down the road 500 yards from the Village.

When the 3 daughters danced into the room with their step-dance costumes and began an entertaining Sunday afternoon, we knew we were in a special place. You might not see the dance, but you'll have a jovial time with the Kerins family. This modern country home not only overlooks the peaceful Kilcolgan River, but has a view of Dunguaire Castle, where medieval banquets are served. The rooms, decorated in pink, rose, and lavender, are comfortable and modern; some have a view of the river. Breakfast is full Irish cooked with fruit, brown bread, porridge, and yogurts. The hearty breakfast is served at a large family table. The lounge with a TV and fire is comfortable and has pleasant views from large bay windows. Martin can put you on to some fine fishing trips. There are salmon and trout in the river. The welcoming is warm and genuine and they proudly point out that Maureen O'Hara stayed there in 1993. The country setting is pretty enough to paint. One of Ireland's best seafood restaurants is down the road—it's called Moran's. Galway Bay golf is next door and sailing and horseback riding are nearby.

Clareview House
Brenda McTigue
Kinvara, County Galway
Telephone: 091-637170
Bedrooms: 5, all with private baths.
Rates: £17.50 p.p.; Single £5 extra; discounts for children. Vouchers accepted. £14 dinner. **Credit cards:** None. **Open:** March 17 to October 31. **Children:** All ages. **Pets:** No. **Smoking:** No. **Provision for handicapped:** No. **Directions:** From the town of Kinvara, go north to Dunguaire Castle, take the road on the right, and go 3 km. The farm is on the left.

This 1890s, 2-story, white farmhouse is set back behind gates on lovely grounds with flower gardens. It is a 120-acre dairy and beef farm. Brenda and her shepherd will greet you and offer you a relaxing tea by the fire in the black marble fireplace. The lounge has a special antique buffet. The rooms are very neat and pretty, done in cream and pink, pale green and cream, and turquoise and off-white, and all the bathrooms are large. All rooms have a great view of the countryside and garden. Brenda's full Irish Breakfast includes homemade black and white pudding. If you reserve ahead, you may have dinner of salmon, trout, or lamb roast for £14 p.p. Since the farm is centrally located, you may go 3 km to the charming town of Kinvara, with its nature walks, shops, colored buildings, nice little restaurants, and fishing boats in the harbor; or to the Dunguaire Castle, where there is a very popular medieval banquet and show, all reserved. There is a 9-hole golf course 10 miles south in Gort; Coole Park with wildlife in Gort; the Burren and Ailwee Caves just south of Kinvara; boat trips, fishing, and swimming at Traught Beach just north; and you'll be only 15 miles from Galway City and 30 miles from Lahinch and the Cliffs of Moher.

Ard Mhuire
Pat and Teresa McDonagh
Knocknacarra Road
Salthill, County Galway
Telephone: 091-522344; **FAX:** 091-529629
Bedrooms: 6, all with private baths, plus separate full bath.
Rates: £17 p.p.; Single £22; 25 percent discount for children under 12.
Vouchers accepted. **Credit cards:** None. **Open:** All year, except Christmas week. **Children:** Yes. **Pets:** No. **Smoking:** No. **Provision for handicapped:** Yes. **Directions:** Go out along the water from city center, along Promenade where Leisureland is located on your right, toward Barna. When you get to Spinnaker House Hotel on the left, the next right is Knocknacarra Road. Ard Mhuire is in the second block on the left, a white home with Spanish arches in front and a white wall surrounding the car park.

This charming modern home has a nice ambience. Rooms are spacious and nicely decorated. Floral grey and white, pale apricot and green, and pink rose are used in an elegant manner. You don't feel crowded in this home as in some B&Bs. The tiled baths are extralarge in 4 of the rooms; some have tubs and showers. All combinations of beds are available, from twins to doubles to triples, so if you reserve early you should get the right accommodations. The gorgeous honeymoon suite with a view of the sea has a king-sized bed with an inset classic archway above, a bright floral-print bedcover, and blue-green walls—very nice! The breakfast menu is a full Irish Breakfast served at a large antique, hand-carved table and chairs or at separate small side tables. The large lounge adjoins the dining area. Mrs. McDonagh is a pleasant hostess who makes you feel right at home and whom we enjoyed chatting with over tea and homemade scones.

Carraig Beag
Catherine Lydon
1 Burren View Heights
Salthill, County Galway
Telephone: 091-521696
Bedrooms: 4, all with private baths.
Rates: £16-18 p.p. (raceweek—£18); Single £25-32; ⅓ discount for children. Vouchers not accepted. **Credit cards:** None. **Open:** All year, except Christmas week. **Children:** Yes. **Pets:** Yes. **Smoking:** Restricted. **Provision for handicapped:** Rooms available on first floor. **Directions:** Past the golf course, take the second road on the right across from Spinnaker. The Cottage Shop is at the corner. Go up Knocknacarra to the corner of Burren View Heights; the house is the first on the right.

Pretty flowers adorn the front of this modern brick home with its look of a stately manor house. It is even more attractive inside with its handsome wood doors, broad staircase, and elegant large dining room with crystal chandelier, adjoining a large living room with marble fireplace for relaxing. Guests have a cozy separate lounge with a TV. The spacious rooms are handsomely decorated in pinks and whites, green and greys, and wine colors, all with their own pretty bathrooms. Some have views. Breakfast is served on a large lace-covered table where you can even view the water through the living room. Breakfast is a full Irish cooked one with home-baked goods and fruit. Catherine Lydon is gracious and dignified yet a charming and friendly hostess who will make your stay in Galway a pleasant and memorable one. She will be quite willing to guide you to the best places for walks, golfing, horseback riding, fishing, or short trips, such as to the Aran Islands, Connemara, or the Burren. She will even tell you about the special sights and traditional music in Galway.

The Connaught
Colette and Tom Keaveney
Barna Road
Salthill, County Galway
Telephone: 091-525865; **FAX:** 091-525865
Bedrooms: 6; 5 with private baths, 1 with shared.
Rates: £17.50 p.p. private bath; £17 shared bath; Single £18; 25 percent discount for children under 12. Vouchers accepted. **Credit cards:** None. **Open:** March 17 to October 31. **Children:** All ages. **Pets:** No. **Smoking:** No. **Provision for handicapped:** No. **Directions:** Drive west along the water (on the Promenade, or R336) from Galway Town and continue through Salthill until you pass the golf club. Turn left at Knocknacarra Cross onto Barna Road. The Connaught is 600 yards on the right.

This is a bright and cheerful Georgian home, probably made so by the Keaveneys. It has a modern exterior and handsome interior. Good-sized bedrooms, all on the second floor, are done in soft pastel colors and are furnished with twin or double beds (some triples), electric blankets, and nice mirrors. There is access to a large balcony facing Rusheen Bay from two of the rooms. This is nice for lounging in the sun. Downstairs is a cozy, pink and brown guest lounge with a TV and stone fireplace. Breakfast is a full Irish cooked one with homemade brown bread and possibly some other pastries, fruit on the buffet, and fresh brewed coffee, served at separate tables. Tom teaches baking and confectionary at a local college, so he provides some added treats to the menu such as his famous croissants. After this hearty breakfast, you can play golf at a nearby championship 18-hole course or go for some water fun at the indoor pool down the road at Leisureland. This young couple is very likeable.

Marian Lodge
Mrs. Celine Molloy
Knocknacarra Road
Salthill, County Galway
Telephone: 091-521678; **FAX:** 091-528103
Bedrooms: 6, all with private baths.
Rates: £16-20 p.p.; Single £20-30; ⅓ discount for children. Vouchers not accepted. **Credit cards:** All major ones. **Open:** All year, except Christmas. **Children:** Yes. **Pets:** No. **Smoking:** Restricted. **Provision for handicapped:** None. **Directions:** Travel along the water (on the Promenade, or R336) from Galway to Salthill; pass Leisureland on the right. Across from Spinnaker turn right on Knocknacarra Road. The 2-story home is on the left, with a sign above the wall to the right of the driveway.

The smell of fresh-baked goods greets you as you enter Marian Lodge. You will receive an especially warm welcome from Celine when you arrive. She and her husband, Pat, are very friendly and most anxious to please. This is a cozy and restful place with lots of good food and comfortable rooms with orthopedic beds, TVs, and tea- and coffee-making facilities. Rooms are decorated in blues, greens, and pinks, with reading lights over the beds and many combinations of beds to suit the traveling public. Some rooms have showers and large tubs in the bathrooms. The living room or lounge has a TV and a brick fireplace with old antique pots and a barrel of peat for burning. Celine tells how her house was built quite recently with solid concrete walls so as to keep it quiet inside. Breakfast is the traditional Irish one and includes fresh-baked scones and soda bread. They have tickets here for deep-sea fishing and windsurfing. They are close to a 22-hole golf course, swimming at Leisureland, horseback riding, and a bus to the Aran Islands. They have private car parking.

Marless House
Mary Geraghty
Threadneedle Road
Salthill, County Galway
Telephone: 091-523931; **FAX:** 091-529810
Bedrooms: 6, all with private baths.
Rates: £18 p.p.; Single £22; 25 percent discount for children under 12.
Vouchers accepted. **Credit cards:** All major ones. **Open:** All year,
except Christmas week. **Children:** Yes. **Pets:** No. **Smoking:** No. **Provision for handicapped:** None. **Directions:** Take the street along the
water from Galway Town, past Leisureland. About 2 km from Galway,
turn right on Threadneedle Road. The B&B is on the right, a pretty,
Georgian 2-story, with a brick front, white pedimented entrance, and
white sides.

This beautiful, modern Georgian brick home is spacious and decorated with fine woodwork and bright colors. Mary is a generous and
kind hostess and spends a lot of time with guests. Her attention to
details and good management results in a pleasant stay. She jokes
that her husband, Tom, who cooks on weekends, is her "honeydew"
husband: "Honey, do this, and honey, do that." We were impressed
with the comfort, size, and decor of our bedroom and bathroom. Our
room was a bright cheery yellow and white. You can have your breakfast on the large dining-room table, if you like to chat with fellow travelers, or at separate tables, if you want privacy. The juice, fruit, cereal,
and yogurt are self-service on the side buffet. Delicious hot entrées
and beverage orders are brought to your table. The living room is
warmly decorated in apricot and blue-green with a white fireplace.
Mary encourages guests to walk the Promenade along the beautiful
Galway Bay, or indulge in the many recreational activities such as golf,
swimming, or tennis.

Ardmore Country House
Vera Feeney
Greenhill
Spiddal, County Galway
Telephone: 091-553145; **FAX:** 091-553596
Bedrooms: 7, all with private baths.
Rates: £17.50-19.50 p.p.; Single £25; discount for children. Vouchers accepted. **Credit cards:** All major ones. **Open:** March through December. **Children:** All ages. **Pets:** No. **Smoking:** Restricted. **Provision for handicapped:** Yes, in "Guide to Handicapped." **Directions:** Go out to Spiddal from Galway Town, through Barna on R336. It is 8 miles to Spiddal (10 miles from city center). The house is ½ mile west of Spiddal town on the left.

This lovely modern home, surrounded by a beautifully landscaped garden, boasts a panoramic view of the bay and the Burren beyond. Vera Feeney is a very well organized, experienced, and gracious hostess who runs one of our favorite B&Bs. She will even arrange a trip to the Aran Islands from Rossaveel. The laundry facilities for weary guests are very popular. The blue or pink bedrooms are very trim and comfortable. Each has 2 or 3 beds with a vanity and sink in separate alcoves, in addition to a private, tiled bathroom. We enjoyed the huge dining/living room with a fireplace for Vera's award-winning breakfasts, and the delightful chats with other guests on the comfy sofas. Rollicking traditional music can be heard in Spiddal town at Hughes Pub almost every night, but be prepared for cramped quarters and lots of smoke. There are plenty of good restaurants in Spiddal so you don't have to go into Galway Town. Budget-priced and very good meals are available in the Bridge House Hotel. We enjoyed the *Bolvisce* restaurant for its coziness and great seafood. Activities available here are fishing, riding, golf, watersports, and swimming at safe sandy beaches within walking distance, and bus tours to Connemara. Excellent bargains can be found at Standum Handcraft Shop in Spiddal.

ALSO RECOMMENDED

Annaghdown, *Corrib View Farm,* Mary Scott Furey. 3 km off Galway-Headford-Castlebar N84 road. Telephone: 091-79114. Bedrooms: 5, 3 with private baths. Open April 5 to September 30. Charming 1890s farmhouse. Regional award winner 1992. Working livestock farm.

Clifden, *Winnowing Hill,* Mrs. Margaret Kelly, Ballyconneely Road. Telephone: 095-21281. Bedrooms: 6, 2 with private baths. Pretty modern country home with views of Clifden village and the Twelve Needles Mountains.

Gort, *Teac Seamus,* Una McCotter, Galway Road. Telephone: 091-31884. Bedrooms: 4, 3 en suite. Quaint thatched-roof cottage on N18, just outside town. Convenient to travelers to and from Galway Town.

Maam Cross (Connemara area), *Tullaboy House,* Mrs. Iris Joyce. Telephone: 091-82305. Bedrooms: 4, all with private baths. Home cooking and hospitality their specialty. Peacocks Restaurant here used in filming of *Quiet Man.*

Oughterard, *Ashlawn House,* Mrs. Mary C. Flaherty, Ardvarna, on N59 near lake. Telephone: 091-82349. Bedrooms: 3, 2 with private baths. Vouchers accepted. Open April to September. Modern home with beautiful gardens.

Oughterard, *Avondale House,* Mrs. Brid Kelly, Portacaron, near Lough Corrib (turn left off the N59 going south at the edge of town). Telephone: 091-82398. Bedrooms: 5, 4 with private baths. Open April to November. Comfortable modern bungalow on quiet country lane. Fishing and boating available.

Oughterard, *Corrib Wave House,* Maria and Michael Healy, Connemara (located 2 miles east of Oughterard off the N59). Telephone: 091-82147. Bedrooms: 8, 6 with private baths. Lakeside farmhouse with panoramic view. Boats, engines, and boatmen available for hire.

Salthill, *Roncalli House,* Tim and Carmel O'Halloran, 24 Whitestrand Ave. Telephone: 091-64159. Bedrooms: 6, all with private baths. A favorite of many travelers. Recommended by Josephine Martin of Mount Royd country home, Carrigans, County Donegal.

COUNTY KERRY

County Kerry

County Kerry is a wonderful blend of purple mountains, green pastures, sea cliffs, smooth beaches, old castles, ancient ruins, and history. Dingle, our favorite town in Ireland, still retains the flavor of a small traditional town in spite of all the tourists who flock there in summer. You'll hear Gaelic spoken in shops and pubs and all street signs are in both Gaelic and English. Gaelic sounds like Danish or Norwegian.

The beauty and serenity of blue Dingle Bay dominates the town. It is still a fishing village, so you may go to the docks of Dingle and watch them unload fish. In summer, you'll note young folks rowing or racing black curraghs (boats made of treated skins). The Slieve Mish Mountains in the background are impressive. Buildings all a different color, stairstepping up the hilly main street, make a beguiling scene.

We found some good sales in the shops, and we were satisfied each time we visited The Forge Restaurant. A favorite lunch place is An Cafe Litearta, a bookstore with a café in the rear that serves everything including decaf coffee, great soups, and hot scones. O'Flaherty's Pub is where you go for music. Some summer nights the walls bend in and out with the rollicking crowds. Try the beach in Ventry or travel down the road to the beach at Inch for swimming and sunning. Connor Pass is a wonder to the eye—you feel like you're on top of a magical green world, with wonderful water views on each side.

Be sure and take the ride out to Slea Head to see the Blasket Islands, where fishermen lived until 1953. Read the book called *Peig*, by the last woman to live there. It tells of the hardship of their lives. Take the steep walk down to the boat ramp; it's invigorating. Notice the miles of stonewalled sheep pens right down to the sea. Go inland a bit and visit some of the ancient beehive houses made of stones, and the old stone church, St. Malcathair, built in the 600s. The stones are all pale lavender, green, blue, pink, and gold.

Tralee is a charming town. It has a show called Siamsa Tire, put on by the National Folk Theatre of Ireland, that is a winner. The show is full of colorful music, dancing, and mime, so it doesn't matter that it's in Gaelic—you'll understand it all. There is a festival every September that features a "Rose of Tralee," chosen from any country in the world.

Killarney is the biggest tourist town of Kerry and it has plenty to offer. Visit the soft lakes of Killarney; take a jaunting car ride to Muckross House or Abbey. The funny drivers have surely kissed the Blarney Stone. Don't forget to see the Gap of Dunloe. The hotels have great Irish musical shows and there are many good Irish singing pubs. Northwest of Killarney, if you hit it just right in August you'll catch the Puck Fair in Killorglin with plenty of step dancing and horse trading. Supposedly it's the oldest fair in Ireland. The Mill Inn in Ballyvourney (in County Cork) has the best lunch between Killarney and Macroom.

The Ring of Kerry in the south provides a thrilling ride around the outer rim of the Iveragh Peninsula. You'll see lovely farms and breathtaking sea views from high cliffs.

Beenoskee Bed and Breakfast
Mary and Michael Ferriter
Cappateige, Connor Pass Road
Castlegregory, County Kerry
Telephone: 066-39263; **FAX:** 066-39263
Bedrooms: 4; 3 with private baths, 1 with shared.
Rates: £15-17 p.p.; 50 percent discount for children. Vouchers
accepted. £13 dinner. **Credit cards:** Yes. **Open:** All year. **Children:** All
ages. **Pets:** No. **Smoking:** Ask owner. **Provision for handicapped:**
None. **Directions:** From Tralee, take the Connor Pass Road. Beenos-
kee is one mile west of Stradbally Village, overlooking Brandon Bay
Beach.

This luxurious, spacious, pink bungalow sits on a hill overlooking
Brandon Bay and is surrounded by beautiful mountains. Mary will
treat you with warm hospitality and will serve you complimentary tea
or coffee and homemade cake. The rooms are nicely situated and decorated, and they have a spectacular view of the seafront, beaches, and
mountains. Mary serves an extensive breakfast menu, including traditional Irish. Evening meals are offered with fresh vegetables and delicious home baking. In the area, there are archaeological sites, a
heritage center, and museums to visit. There are tranquil walks, surfing, golf, horseback riding, mountain climbing, fishing, windsurfing,
and swimming nearby. This home is centrally located between Tralee
and Dingle on the beautiful Connor Pass Road.

The Shores Country House
Annette O'Mahoney
Cappatigue, Connor Pass Road
Castlegregory, County Kerry
Telephone: 066-39196
Bedrooms: 3, all with private baths.
Rates: £17-20 p.p.; Single £5 extra; 33 percent discount for children.
Vouchers accepted. £16 dinner. **Credit cards:** VISA. **Open:** March 17
to November 17. **Children:** All ages. **Pets:** No. **Smoking:** No. **Provision for handicapped:** None. **Directions:** From Tralee, follow Dingle
Road for about 10 miles to the first junction, take a right turn to Dingle via Connor Pass. Go 10 miles, and you will see the Shores Country House. If you need further directions, please call the owner.

This family-run inn off in the country is a great getaway for city
folks. Overlooking the longest beach in Ireland, it has landscaped gardens; and Mount Brandon is in the mountain range just behind the
house. The oak, pine, and blue rooms all have wonderful sea views
and handsome antiques. One is sand color, burgundy, gold, and
green. Other rooms are decorated with white wicker and porcelain
dolls. The sitting room is divided from the dining room with marble
columns, and it is decorated in soft peaches and greys. Annette greets
you with tea and homemade porter cake. Her breakfasts are full Irish,
or scrambled eggs and smoked salmon, fresh fruit and yogurt, waffles, croissants, and Irish farmhouse cheese. Annette will pack a lunch
for you. Her gourmet dinners, featuring fresh salmon, chicken, lamb,
or cod and great desserts, are on a menu. They hope to have 4 new
rooms added by 1998. Mountain walks are nearby and the beach is
only 10 minutes away.

Murphy's Farmhouse
The Murphy Family
Boolteens
Castlemaine, County Kerry
Telephone: 066-67337; **FAX:** 066-67839
Bedrooms: 14; 13 with private baths, 1 with shared.
Rates: £16 p.p.; Single £18; 50 percent discount for children under 12, under 2 free. Vouchers accepted. £12, 5-course dinner; £7, just main course. **Credit cards:** None. **Open:** All year. **Children:** Yes. **Pets:** Reasonable size. **Smoking:** Yes. **Provision for handicapped:** None. **Directions:** The farmhouse is 2 miles from Castlemaine town. Take the Dingle road west to Boolteens. A sign will be on the right. Follow the road to the end. There are also signs in Castlemaine and Brackhill Cross.

This lovely farm B&B situated on the south flank of the Slieve Mish Mountains was first discovered by us in 1984, and still is a great place to stay. It has been in the family since 1847. When we were at Murphy's, we went to the Puck Fair in Killorglin, originally a pagan country fair where a goat rules as king, and we enjoyed swimming at nearby Inch Beach. At the farm the meals are delicious. The full Irish Breakfast, augmented with kippers and various cheeses, and the tasty farm dinners are served in the newly decorated dining room. All the bedrooms have been redecorated with flowered wallpaper and new bedcovers, and now have tea- and coffee-making facilities, electric blankets, and electric heaters. The roses and ivy in front, set against the pink house with white trim, make it look like a picture postcard. The cozy and spacious lounge, with a fireplace and TV, provides a good opportunity to visit with the many other guests. We found many Irish guests here who come every year. The Murphy family all pitches in to make your stay here at their ancestral dairy farm a pleasant one. There are golf courses nearby.

Ard Na Greine House
Mary and Michael Houlihan
Spa Road
Dingle, County Kerry
Telephone: 066-51113; **FAX:** 066-51898
Bedrooms: 4, all with private baths.
Rates: £16-18 p.p.; no discount for children. Vouchers accepted.
Credit cards: VISA and MasterCard. **Open:** All year. **Children:** Yes, 7
years and older. **Pets:** No. **Smoking:** No. **Provision for handicapped:**
None. **Directions:** When entering Dingle from Tralee or Killarney,
turn right at the roundabout onto The Mall road. Continue straight
through at the next intersection; this is Spa Road. Stay to the left at the
Hill Grove Hotel. Ard Na Greine is on the left.

This attractive pink bungalow in a quiet location within walking distance of the village center is highly recommended by many other
B&Bs and the British A.A. and R.A.C. All bedrooms have a TV with
satellite channels, refrigerator, direct-dial telephone, electric blankets,
tea- and coffee-making facilities, an iron, and ironing board. So you
can see you will be fully equipped to enjoy this popular town in comfort and style. Breakfast features the smoked salmon or herring, and
homemade breads with the full Irish Breakfast. The advantage to this
B&B is that you receive a quality bed and breakfast, and you will be
within walking distance of pubs with excellent traditional music and
the great restaurants of Dingle. Up the road is Connor Pass, and of
course, a trip around Slea Head is a must.

Ard-na-Mara Country House
Mrs. Ann Murphy
Ballymore, Ventry
Dingle, County Kerry
Telephone: 066-59072
Bedrooms: 4, all with private baths.
Rates: £16 p.p.; Single £18; 50 percent discount for children under 12.
Vouchers accepted. £12 dinner on request or £10 for 2 nights. **Credit
cards:** None. **Open:** March 17 to November 15. **Children:** All ages.
Pets: No. **Smoking:** Restricted. **Provision for handicapped:** None.
Directions: From Dingle, go by the harbor, continue to the bridge,
and then go left toward Slea Head Drive. On the left, 2 miles from
the bridge, look for the sign. Turn left toward the water.

This modern home overlooking scenic Ventry Harbor is nicely situated on the R559 for your tour of the Dingle Peninsula. Ann gives
you a warm welcome with tea and cookies when you arrive. All the
rooms have duvets with tiny green prints and matching curtains. Doubles, twins, and triples are available. All rooms have tea- and coffee-
making facilities, hairdryers, and alarm/clock radios. The lounge is a
large living room with a fireplace, TV, and piano, so if you'd like an
Irish singalong this is your place. A breakfast menu is provided, which
allows you to choose your breakfast. We noted that French toast,
yogurt, fruit and cheese, and other tasty items were included, which
will allow you to have a change from the usual cooked breakfast. The
chairs in front allow visitors to relax and survey the majestic seacoast
beyond. Ann has served for groups of watercolor painters from the
U.S. who have come with master artists to do landscape and seascape
painting. It is just that beautiful here, and the Murphys are great hosts.

Cleevaun
Sean and Charlotte Cluskey
Lady's Cross
Dingle, County Kerry
Telephone and **FAX:** 066-51108
Bedrooms: 9; 5 with private baths, 4 with shared (standard).
Rates: £25 p.p. private bath; £22 shared bath; Single £10 extra; 10 percent discount for children. **Credit cards:** All except AMEX. **Open:** March to mid-December. **Children:** Yes, older than 8. **Pets:** Only guide dogs. **Smoking:** No. **Provision for handicapped:** None. **Directions:** Take the roundabout (R559) in Dingle toward Slea Head Drive. Follow the signs, keeping the water on the left. Go left over the bridge toward Ventry. After about 500 yards, the house is on the left with a fence and beautifully landscaped garden in front surounding the car park.

Cleevaun is one of our favorites. We have been here for many visits, even before the Cluskeys bought it. We love the panoramic view from the dining room of fields with sheep, Dingle Bay in the distance, and the Eask Tower on the hill protecting the harbor. There is a large ancient burial stone in the field behind the house as well as some underground tunnels that may have connected some beehive houses. The country pine woodwork of the downstairs corner room, with the green bedcover and drapes, is very attractive, as are the rest of the rooms, all with pine furniture and matching bedspreads. In fact, this lovely house is very nice inside and out, and a good "base camp" from which to expore the Dingle Peninsula, see the Gallarus Oratory, St. Kilmalkedar, and other Christian antiquities. Charlotte Cluskey will cook you a wonderful full Irish Breakfast with many choices of eggs, fruit, yogurt, Irish cheese, pancakes, muffins, scones, good jams, and fresh-brewed coffee, including decaffeinated. She won the 1994 Galtee Breakfast of the Year Award. She has an extensive library in the lounge, which describes the history and sights of the Dingle Peninsula and includes loads of books to browse through. This B&B is rated by the British RAC and AA.

Cluain Mhuire House
Mrs. Margaret Noonan
Spa Road
Dingle, County Kerry
Telephone: 066-51291
Bedrooms: 5, all with private baths, plus extra full baths.
Rates: £16 p.p.; Single £20; 20 percent discount for children under 12.
Vouchers accepted. **Credit cards:** All major ones. **Open:** All year. **Children:** Yes. **Pets:** Yes. **Smoking:** Restricted to lounge. **Provision for handicapped:** None. **Directions:** At the roundabout in Dingle go right and follow the sign to Cluain Mhuir, as if going to Connor Pass. It is the next B&B after Hillgrove Hotel.

This comfy cozy B&B is hosted by a lovely lady who will take care of your every need. Attractive rooms with 2 doubles or double and single are available. There are nice lounge chairs and umbrellas in the front garden and the house has a beautiful view of fields and mountains. In the living room there is a beautiful, large fireplace made with colored stone from Minard Castle. The bedrooms are all carpeted and pretty, with TVs, electric blankets, hairdryers, irons, and tea-making facilities. She serves a standard Irish cooked breakfast with choice of cereals and juice, but yogurts, fruit, fish, beans, or a cold plate are also served. Hot Barry tea and fresh scones were rolled out for a nice Irish welcome when we visited Mrs. Noonan's traditional Irish home. There is a soccer table game in the dinng room and some musical instruments. Take a 5-minute walk into Dingle for shops and restaurants.

The Half Door
Denis and Teresa O'Connor
Mail Road
Dingle, County Kerry
Telephone and **FAX:** 066-51883
Bedrooms: 7, all with private baths.
Rates: £17-25 p.p.; no charge for children under 4. £15.50 dinner.
Credit cards: VISA. **Open:** All year. **Children:** Yes. **Pets:** No. **Smoking:**
Restricted. **Provision for handicapped:** None. **Directions:** It is the first
B&B on the right as you enter town, set back with pine trees on each
side and overlooking the bay. Look for a yellow house with a red door.

This friendly couple will greet you at the door and welcome you to
their pretty, new, 3-story bed and breakfast. It is bright yellow with a
red door and has a view of Dingle Bay. The rooms are modern, decorated in pastel pink and white with floral drapes and lovely matching
rugs and duvets. Baths are spacious with fully tiled showers. A beautiful bedroom on the first floor has a fireplace and view of the bay. The
sitting room has a fireplace and TV. Breakfast is standard Irish Breakfast with other specialties like smoked salmon on a croissant, bacon,
fish cakes, poached eggs, all preceded by brown bread and a medley of
fruit. You can walk to town and shop and visit the many excellent
restaurants in Dingle, including our favorite, The Forge, which Teresa
can direct you to. Another good one is The Half Door Restaurant
owned by the O'Connors. The best music is at O'Flaherty's Pub. Dingle is supposed to have the most 4-star restaurants in Ireland. Play
golf 8 miles away at Ballyferriter, ride horseback at the youth hostel,
and play tennis in Dingle. Drive out to Slea Head to see the Blasket
Islands and local potters, or visit the beehive houses and ancient stone
church just beyond Dingle going west. You'll need explicit directions
from your hosts.

Rockcrest House
Marian and David O'Dwyer
Gortamullen
Kenmare, County Kerry
Telephone: 064-41248
Bedrooms: 6, all with private baths.
Rates: £17 p.p.; Single £17; 33 percent discount for children. Vouchers accepted. £13 dinner. **Credit cards:** All major ones. **Open:** All year. **Children:** All ages. **Pets:** Yes. **Smoking:** Yes. **Provision for handicapped:** None. **Directions:** Heading south just outside Kenmare town center, there is a sign posted for Rockcrest House off of N71 Killarny road (on the outskirts of Kenmare town).

Rockcrest House is an elegant, dormer-style guesthouse on a quiet, scenic location overlooking the prehistoric site of a dolmen stone circle and the Kenmore River Valley. A beautiful rock garden and stone wall adorn the entrance to the house. All six rooms are spacious and nicely decorated. They have TVs, hairdryers, and other facilities. Most have views of the lovely countryside. There is a 13th-century bridge, the stone circle, and a holy well, all within 800 yards of the house. Marian and David O'Dwyer serve a full Irish Breakfast in their attractive dining room, and dinner is offered if booked ahead. Babysitting is offered until midnight. Nearby you'll find golf, horseback riding, walking (including a guided hill walk), fishing, boat trips, and all watersports on the Kenmare River. The house is only a 5-minute walk from the town of Kenmare with its good restaurants and pubs.

Whispering Pines
John and Mary Fitzgerald
Bellheight
Kenmare, County Kerry
Telephone: 064-41194
Bedrooms: 4, all with private baths.
Rates: £18 p.p.; Single £20; 50 percent discount for children under 12. Vouchers accepted. **Credit cards:** None. **Open:** March 1 to November 1. **Children:** Yes, ages 5 and up. **Pets:** No. **Smoking:** Restricted to lounge. **Provision for handicapped:** Yes. **Directions:** From the center of Kenmare take Glengarriff Road south. Go about ½ mile from the center of town, but before the harbor on the right is Whispering Pines, pink with white trim.

This pretty 1914 home decorated inside with beautiful pastel colors is a wonderful place to stay. It is located on the edge of town, set behind a lovely garden. John and Mary give you a warm welcome to their home. The 4 spacious and handsomely decorated rooms, all with private baths, are painted in soft colors with matching borders—one in black and pink roses, another with peach walls and matching pink flowered duvets. The home has a comfy, restful feeling. The dining room is spacious with separate tables. Breakfast is a hearty Irish cooked meal with homemade brown bread. Dry cereals are available with fruit and other provisions for those who want vegetarian or lighter fare. There is an arched front hall and a nice sitting room with a marble fireplace and TV. A 9-hole golf course and a riding stable are nearby for reasonable fees. We walked to town one night and watched a caeli. A caeli is a Gaelic amateur-night singalong or dance done in the pubs or local hotels. Kenmare is a quaint town by the sea, not as busy and full of tourists as Killarney, yet more preferred by many.

Brookside
Anne and Neilius Moriarty
Gortacollopa, Fossa
Killarney, County Kerry
Telephone: 064-44187
Bedrooms: 6, all with private baths; plus a 3-bedroom housekeeping cottage with fireplace.
Rates: £17 p.p.; Single £19.50; 25 percent discount for children. Vouchers accepted. £13 dinner. **Credit cards:** None. **Open:** March 1 to November 7. **Children:** All ages. **Pets:** Negotiable. **Smoking:** No. **Provision for handicapped:** Limited. **Directions:** From Killarney, take the N72 (R562), follow the signpost to Hotel Europe. Brookside is two miles farther, on the right side of the road, next to Kerry Die Products.

This handsome bungalow on the outskirts of busy Killarney is in a quiet pastoral area with a lovely flower garden in front. Anne and Neilius are very gracious and generous with their time and show guests the best way to appreciate their wonderful town. Neilius is now the head of Killarney's Chamber of Commerce. The bedrooms are decorated in pastel pinks, peach, and green with handmade duvets and matching drapes in flowered materials. Some rooms have views of hills with grazing sheep and ponies. Brookside was awarded the Country Rover Irish B&B of the year in 1993 and 1994. The sitting room with turf fire is a social center of this home where tea is served. Breakfast varies from the full Irish one to choices of smoked salmon, beans on toast, scrambled eggs, poached eggs with bacon, cheese and tomato, fruit, yogurt, tea, coffee, and hot chocolate. This home is 4 miles from Killarney with its jaunting cart trips, Gap of Dunloe, boating on the lakes, golf, cycling, ponytrekking, and a bus to the Ring of Kerry. Your stay will be a memorable one, with the Moriartys indulging your every need.

Carrowmore House
Pat and Kathleen McAuliffe
Knockasarnett
Aghadoe
Killarney, County Kerry
Telephone: 064-33520
Bedrooms: 5, all with private baths.
Rates: £17 p.p.; Single £23; 25 percent discount for children. Vouchers not accepted. **Credit cards:** None. **Open:** April 1 to October 31. **Children:** All ages. **Pets:** No. **Smoking:** Restricted. **Provision for handicapped:** None. **Directions:** Take the N22 north on the Killarney, Tralee, Limerick Road. The house is about 2 km from Killarney town.

Set in a tranquil area with beautiful panoramic view, this bed and breakfast comes highly recommended by other hosts in our book. The bedrooms are spacious, done in rust and cream, peach and brown, pink and blue, and other fashionable colors. All rooms have color-coordinated carpets, linens, and curtains with the color scheme continued in the en suite bathrooms. Breakfast is the full Irish cooked one with eggs any style, both puddings, and grilled tomato. Juice and hot/cold cereals are also served. Save room though for the home-baked bread, and sultana scones. For recreation there is horseback riding, golf, and fishing locally. Pat and Kathleen can arrange local tours from the Carrowmore House.

Coffey's Loch Lein Guest House
Eithne Coffey
Golf Course Road, Fossa
Killarney, County Kerry
Telephone: 064-31260; **FAX:** 064-36151
Bedrooms: 12, all with private baths.
Rates: £18-25 p.p.; Single £25-30; 50 percent discount for children.
Vouchers accepted. **Credit cards:** VISA, MasterCard, Access. **Open:**
March to November. **Children:** All ages. **Pets:** No. **Smoking:** Restricted.
Provision for handicapped: Yes. **Directions:** From Killarney Center
take Killorglin Road for 3 miles. Past Hotel Europe on the left and
Prince of Peace Church. Take the next left on Golf Course Road. Fol-
low the signs to Coffey's Loch Lein.

This spacious, very comfortable, and neat guesthouse, just outside
Killarney among beautiful old trees with a large front garden, is made
special by Eithne Coffey with her energetic and humorous style. It is
situated by Killarney's lower lake with the mountains rising up to the
south, a pretty vista from the lounge and dining room. Snow was on
the mountains in May when we were there. All of the rooms have been
tastefully decorated and are very comfortable with large private baths.
We liked the guesthouse because it is off the main road, set back, and
free from the hustle and bustle of downtown Killarney. There are
many things to do in Killarney, including the nearby golfing, tennis,
boating, fishing, hiking, and horseback riding. A Dublin hiking club
was there when we were at the guesthouse; they were ready to hike the
snow-covered MacGillycuddy's Reeks. A delight for many is the trip up
the nearby Gap of Dunloe in a pony trap, and stopping for a pint
after at the pub, Kate Kearney's, near the entrance. A pint before will
make the scenery even rosier. This is one of our favorite guesthouses
because of the relaxed atmosphere and the charm of the Coffeys.

The Grotto
Joan and Jerry Ryan
Fossa
Killarney, County Kerry
Telephone: 064-33283
Bedrooms: 6, all with private baths.
Rates: £16.50 p.p.; 50 percent discount for children under 12. Vouchers accepted. **Credit cards:** Yes. **Open:** March 1 through November 30.
Children: All ages. **Pets:** Yes. **Smoking:** Restricted. **Provision for handicapped:** Yes. **Directions:** Take Killorglin Road (R565—Ring of Kerry/Dingle road). The home is just a few yards beyond Castlerosse Hotel and before the entrance to the Golf Club.

A pretty garden greets you as you enter the gate to this beautiful modern country home. The spacious bedrooms with dressing tables are done in Laura Ashley style with colors of peach/cream, grey/pink, and blue/grey, each with its own with tea- and coffee-making facilities. The dining room has separate tables with white tablecloths and flowers. There is a cozy lounge with a TV. Breakfast could be a delicious cooked Irish one with eggs and bacon or a ham, cheese, mushroom omelette, or a continental/vegetarian one with cereal, yogurt, cheese, and a variety of fresh fruit. Jerry and Joan are extremely helpful in guiding you to the various tourist sights and activities of Killarney, of which there are many and as diverse as anyplace in Ireland. Killarney's 2 championship golf courses and fishing club are situated opposite The Grotto on the Ring of Kerry/Dingle road. Horseback riding and hill and mountain hiking are some of the other features. The Irish Tourist Board Office in the Killarney town hall (Tel.: 064-31633) can provide you with dates and times of special events in this region. This B&B has been recommended by many other B&B owners and travelers in Ireland.

Lisaden
Betty O'Sullivan
97 Countess Grove
(off) Countess Road
Killarney, County Kerry
Telephone: 064-32006
Bedrooms: 5, all en suite, some triples or family rooms.
Rates: £17 p.p.; 25 percent discount for children. Vouchers accepted.
Credit cards: None. **Open:** March to November. **Children:** Yes. **Pets:**
No. **Smoking:** Restricted to lounge. **Provision for handicapped:** None.
Directions: Call Mrs. O'Sullivan for directions.

This beautiful bungalow was chosen the best town and country home in Killarney in 1994. Surrounded by lovely gardens and shrubbery, it is situated in a quiet area off of the main road that allows you to escape the hustle and bustle of Killarney, which is usually brimful of tourists. All five rooms are done in colorful, pastel shades of pale pinks and off-whites with matching curtains and flowered duvets. They are equipped with tea-making facilities and hairdryers. The lovely, large guest lounge has a TV, a fireplace, and a bass viol. The pretty dining room has individual tables with linen cloths. Breakfast includes full Irish, or continental/vegetarian with fruit yogurt and a choice of cereals. It is only a 7-minute walk to the center of Killarney town, with its great restaurants and tourist sights.

Muckross Lodge
Bernadette O'Sullivan
Muckross Road
Killarney, County Kerry
Telephone and **FAX:** 064-32660
Bedrooms: 5, all with private baths.
Rates: £17.50 p.p.; Single £25 p.p.; 33 percent discount for children.
Vouchers not accepted. **Credit cards:** VISA, MasterCard, Access.
Open: March 15 to October 31. **Children:** Yes. **Pets:** No. **Smoking:**
Restricted. **Provision for handicapped:** None. **Directions:** From Kil-
larney town, follow signs for National Park and Muckross. Muckross
Lodge is near the Eagle Hotel.

This attractive two-story dormer style residence is very close to exciting Killarney town and adjacent to Muckross House Museum and Gardens. Bernadette is a warm and welcoming hostess, and you will find
her beautifully decorated rooms in blues, pinks, and rusts; they are
comfortable with tea- and coffee-making facilities, television, and
hairdryers. In her dining room, she serves a full Irish Breakfast with
additional offerings of homemade scones, fresh fruit salad, yogurt,
cheese, and freshly served coffee. The beautiful Killarney lakes are
nearby, as are traffic-free walking and cycling paths, golf courses, and
coaches to the Ring of Kerry. Pony-trekking is also available at the Gap
of Dunloe, along with jaunting cart rides from Killarney center to
Muckross House. The drivers have a great line of history plus blarney. One guest said Bernadette's hospitality was "superb."

Brook Manor Lodge
Eleanor and Dave Martin
Fenit Road, Spa
Tralee, County Kerry
Telephone: 066-20406; **FAX:** 066-27552
Bedrooms: 6, all with private baths.
Rates: £28-30; Single £30-32; 50 percent discount for children. Vouchers not accepted. **Credit cards:** All major ones. **Open:** March 17 to October 30. **Children:** Yes, over 10. **Pets:** No. **Smoking:** No. **Provision for handicapped:** Yes, 1 room. **Directions:** From Tralee center, take R551 and turn left at R551/R558 junction onto R558 towards Tralee golf course. The house is 2 km from Tralee.

This large, two-story house is "purpose built" on 3.6 acres. It is just outside of Tralee and offers a view of the Slieve Mish Mountains. You will find the Martins are friendly and helpful hosts. The sumptuous rooms are tastefully decorated in navy and white, or pink and white, with Victorian lamps, chairs, and mirrors. Many rooms look out onto private gardens, and all provide television, telephone, tea- and coffee-making facilities, hairdryers, a trouser press, and alarm/clock radio. The breakfast is served in an elegant dining hall by the fireplace or in an adjoining conservatory. Many combinations from the menu are offered, including locally made pork sausages, Irish smoked salmon with fruit or eggs, baked beans or yogurt, cheese and crackers, and freshly made coffee. Afternoon tea is served by the fire in the relaxing guest lounge. Nearby is horseback riding, golf, sailing, and fishing. The beaches are only minutes away. There is the Siamsa Tire show in Tralee, and award-winning seafood restaurants are nearby.

O'Sheas
Mairead O'Shea
2 Oakpark Drive
Tralee, County Kerry
Telephone and **FAX:** 066-80123
Bedrooms: 4, all with private baths.
Rates: £16-20 p.p.; Single £20; discount for children. Vouchers not accepted. **Credit cards:** None. **Open:** May 1 to October 31. **Children:** All ages. **Pets:** Yes. **Smoking:** Restricted. **Provision for handicapped:** None. **Directions:** Turn right at the traffic lights at the railway station, coming from Limerick/Killarney direction. After a 3-minute drive, O'Sheas is on the left side. Look for the sign.

This young, hospitable, and helpful couple will make for a pleasant stay in the area. Fran's sister Carol was especially appreciative of the care Mrs. O'Shea took to give them advice on traveling over Connor Pass during daylight hours. This traditional modern home is cozy with family pictures and fluffy pillows in the living room. There is a satellite TV and a VCR. The carpeted bedrooms are perfect with curtains, lamps, and bedcovers matching with a Victorian flare, individually decorated in light blues, pinks, peaches, and creams. All rooms have radios and orthopedic beds. The breakfast is either the traditional Irish cooked breakfast or the continental. The side buffet has hot and cold cereal, yogurt, fruit, and juice. The home is close to downtown restaurants and Siamsa Tire (the National Folk Theater of Ireland show). Tralee is a good central place from which to visit the Dingle Peninsula and Killarney. It is convenient to beaches, golf courses, Kerry Airport, and the racetrack. The owners of this B&B run a tour bus company called O'Shea's Travel, which does group and individual tours around Ireland and in the U.K. They also do educational tours.

ALSO RECOMMENDED

Dingle, *Bambury's Guest House,* Bernie Bambury, Mail Road. Telephone: 066-51244; FAX: 066-51786. Bedrooms: 12, all with private baths. Modern guesthouse within 2 minutes walking distance of town. Scenic view of harbor from back rooms. Many amenities. Pretty dining room decorated with three green colors. Very good breakfast menu.

Dingle, *Milltown,* John and Angela Gill, just beyond town facing the harbor entrance. Telephone: 066-51372; FAX: 006-51095. Bedrooms: 10, all en suite. Comfortable and well located. 4-star rating from the Irish Tourist Board and highly recommended by many guidebooks.

Dingle, *Sos an Iolair,* Mrs. Mary Moriarity, Ballintlea, Ventry. Telephone: 066-59827. Bungalow in countryside. Small but comfortable bedroom, en suite or private bath and shower suitable only for people of small build, but separate toilet available at end of corridor. Very caring and welcoming couple. Tea/coffee and cookies available whenever requested. Generous draughts of Irish whiskey supplied before one goes out to local reataurant. Recommended to us by Harry McWilliams of Chalfont St. Peter, Buckinghamshire, England.

Kenmare, *Hawthorne House,* Trina and Kevin Murphy. Telephone: 064-41035; FAX: 064-41932. Bedrooms: 8, all with private baths. Lovely gardens surrounding with private car park. Period beds and furniture.

Kenmare, *Mylestone House,* Mrs. Fiona O'Sullivan, Killowen Road. Telephone: 064-41753. Bedrooms: 5, all with private baths. New luxury residence opposite Kenmare Golf Course. Town center 4 minutes away.

Kenmare, *Ocean Wave,* Mrs. Noreen O'Toole, Glenbeigh. Telephone: 066-68249. Bedrooms: 6, all with private baths. On Ring of Kerry near Dooks Golf Course. Specializing in a variety of breakfast items. One that we especially enjoyed. Recommended by Mrs. Helen Callanan of Park View House, Dún Laoghaire, County Dublin.

Killarney, *Gap View Farm,* Mrs. Mary Kearney, Ballyhar. Telephone: 066-64378. Bedrooms: 6, 4 with private baths. 8 miles from Killarney town. Send for their colored brochure. Recommended by our friend Marge Brennan of Gloucester, Mass.

Killarney, *St. Anthony's Villa,* Mrs. Mary Connell, Cork Road. Telephone: 064-31534. Bedrooms: 4, 3 with private baths. Especially nice

B&B in the Cork Road area. Recommended by many travelers and especially by a top Irish historian, Dr. Edna McGlynn.

Killorglin, *Fern Rock,* Mrs. Irma Clifford, Tinnahalla. Telephone: 066-61848. Bedrooms: 4, 3 with private baths. Luxurious residence on N70 with beautiful view. One that we particularly enjoy. Recommended by Monica O'Loughlin of Massabielle, Ennis, County Clare.

Listowel, *Ashgrove House,* Nancy O'Neil, Ballybunion Road. Telephone: 068-21268. Bedrooms: 4, all with private baths. Vouchers accepted. Superb country home adjoining farmlands. Orthopedic beds. Recommended by Vera Feeney, chairman of the Galway Town and Country Homes Association.

Listowel, *Ceol na h' Abhann,* Niall and Kathleen Stack, Ballygrennane. Telephone: 068-21345. Bedrooms: 4, 3 with private baths. Irish National Award winner. Thatched house on river bank. Recommended by many travel guides and also by Catherine Lydon of Carraig Beag, Salthill, County Galway.

Sneem (Ring of Kerry), *Woodvale (Old Convent House),* Mrs. Alice O'Sullivan, Pier Road. Telephone: 064-45181. Bedrooms: 6, all with private baths. All major credit cards. Old-World Tudor house set on own grounds on estuary of Sneem River, overlooked by Direenvourig Mountains.

Tralee, *Seaview House,* Mrs. Bridie Fitzgerald, Main Dingle Road, Annagh, Blennerville. Telephone: 066-21830. Bedrooms: 5, all with private baths. Spacious bungalow in picturesque surroundings, beneath Slieve Mish Mountains. Overlooking Tralee Bay. 4½ miles to Tralee. Recommended by Vera Feeney of Galway.

County Kilkenny

County Kilkenny is strategically located between Cork or Tipperary and Dublin, and it's between Waterford and Dublin, which makes it a natural stopping place. It is also only a little over an hour away from Glendalough in the Wicklow Mountains. The countryside is poetically rural, with many sheep farms and the Nore River flowing through the center of the county adding to its scenic beauty.

Kilkenny Town, although holding well to its medieval history, is worldly. It offers fine cultural features such as the Irish National Design Center across from the castle, built to encourage young crafts-people. It has a showroom where crafts can be bought, and upstairs is a restaurant with delicious, creative meals. Also, good Irish plays are put on at the Watergate Theatre, and there is a cinema in town. You may want to peruse the art galleries and bookstores.

Imposing 13th-century Kilkenny Castle, on the river, is the center of attention in this town. Nicely restored with its 2 enormous turrets on either end, it covers 49 acres including a huge public park with play-grounds for children and attractive gardens. You can tour the castle daily, mid-March to September 30, and on weekends the rest of the year.

Go to the Tourist Information Office at the old Shee Alms House on Rose Inn Street at the bridge and join a tour of the town. With a well-informed guide, you'll take a brisk walk to see the Black Abbey; St. Canice's Cathedral; Kyteler's Inn, which once housed a witch; and "Irish Town."

Kyteler's has a fun restaurant downstairs in cave-like rooms. Get a terrific meal at Edward Langton's at 65 John St. It has a high glass-ceilinged dining room and has won many awards.

For a beautiful tour out of Kilkenny Town, drive south on R700 to Thomastown, Woodstock Forest Park, and Jerpoint Abbey. Visit the grounds of Mount Juliet House, a hotel on 1,400 acres of pastureland with horses grazing. It has an Equestrian Center and Stud Farm.

Continue through the pastoral country to the town of Inistioge, a heavenly village with the town center nestled among hills and a humpy bridge over the river with sheep lying on its banks. Just across from the park is an excellent restaurant for lunch. The fishing is good in this relaxing area. It is also a pretty ride over to Carrick on Suir and Clonmel in Tipperary.

Ashville
Maura Naddy
Kilmacshane
Inistioge, County Kilkenny
Telephone: 056-58460; **FAX:** 056-58418
Bedrooms: 4; 3 with private baths, 1 with shared.
Rates: £16 p.p. private bath; £14 p.p. shared bath; Single £18; 50 per-cent discount for children under 12. Vouchers accepted. **Credit cards:** VISA, Access, Eurocard. **Open:** March 1 to October 31. **Children:** All ages. **Pets:** No. **Smoking:** No. **Provision for handicapped:** None. **Direc-tions:** From Kilkenny city, the B&B is 15 miles southeast on the Ross-lare Road on the right, just north of the town of Inistioge. It is 4 miles south of Thomastown.

This modern grey and white brick bungalow overlooks the beauti-ful Nore Valley and has gardens for visitors to enjoy. Maura is genial as she serves you her welcoming tea. She says she treats her guests "like family." The rooms are cheerful with their colors of red and white, pink and beige, and green and yellow. The lounge and dining room have a lovely view. A full Irish Breakfast is served and you may have din-ner there if you order it ahead. The charming town of Inistioge, where Fran painted one of her favorite scenes of sheep across the river and a pretty arched bridge, is 2 minutes away with a very homey restau-rant right in the square. There is also Woodstock Forest Park, Jerpoint Abbey, fishing in the Nore River, golf, walking, and swimming very nearby. Horseback ride at Mount Juliet, a gorgeous estate, and of course visit the exciting medieval town of Kilkenny.

Nore Valley Villa
Leslie and Lucy Rothwell
Inistioge, County Kilkenny
Telephone and **FAX:** 056-58418
Bedrooms: 4; 2 with private baths, 2 with shared.
Rates: £17 p.p.; Single £20; 20 percent discount for children under 12.
Vouchers accepted. £11 dinner. **Credit cards:** VISA, AMEX. **Open:**
March 1 to November 30. **Children:** All ages. **Pets:** Yes. **Smoking:**
Restricted. **Provision for handicapped:** None. **Directions:** Go south
from Kilkenny 15 miles on the road to New Ross (R700). The house
is just before Inistioge on the right, just a few houses away from
Ashville B&B.

This neo-Georgian-style home, with a vintage garden of flowers and
shrubs, has a wonderful view of the lovely Nore River and its valley.
Leslie and Lucy like to help you find the great historical sites and
other places to visit in the area. All the bedrooms are nicely furnished
and have oversized windows that look out to the scenic and peaceful
river. Breakfast is typical Irish with choices. This house is only ¼ km
from the pretty town of Inistioge with its park by the river and views
of sheep and the humpy bridge from the south, a photographer's or
a painter's dream. It is very close to Mount Juliet, where there is a
stud farm for horses and one can horseback ride through its country
trails. The Rothwells will lead you to the fishing, golf, and hill walks
nearby. Ask them about the local pub "craic" (that's music to you non-
Gaels).

Cnoc Mhuire
Helen and Don Sheehan
Castle Road
Kilkenny Town, County Kilkenny
Telephone: 056-62161
Bedrooms: 4; 3 with private baths, 1 with separate.
Rates: £17 p.p.; Single £22; 50 percent discount for children under 12.
Vouchers accepted. **Credit cards:** None. **Open:** All year, except Christmas week. **Children:** All ages. **Pets:** No. **Smoking:** Restricted to lounge.
Provision for handicapped: Yes. **Directions:** From Kilkenny town center, at the castle take Bennetsbridge Road (Castle Road) to the second B&B sign; go right. The house is the first B&B on the left.

This modern house is run by an enchanting couple, Helen and Don, who really put themselves out to make you comfortable and help you with directions for a good tour of Kilkenny. Their rooms are cozy with peach, pink, and rose colors. All have electric blankets, and the bathrooms are good-sized. There is a separate small lounge with a bay window and TV. The dining room is quite pleasant and there is plenty of tea and coffee in pots with cozies to keep them hot. Don squeezes fresh orange juice every night, and besides the typical Irish Breakfast, you'll be offered lots of homemade scones, yogurt, fresh fruit like grapefruit, and—some days—kippers. It's a great spot as it is just a short walk to town, where you can visit the medieval castle and park with a playground, and walk around the old city of museums, craft shops, and great pubs and restaurants. We have attended the Watergate Theatre and have seen many fine Irish plays. Golf, fishing, and horseback riding are also within 15 minutes' drive. Be sure you visit The Irish National Design Center for good crafts and a wonderful lunch.

Danville House
Kitty Stallard
New Ross Road
Kilkenny, County Kilkenny
Telephone: 056-21512
Bedrooms: 4; 3 with private baths, 1 with shared.
Rates: £17 p.p.; 10 percent discount for children. Vouchers accepted.
Credit cards: None. **Open:** April 1 to October 31. **Children:** All ages.
Pets: No. **Smoking:** No. **Provision for handicapped:** None. **Directions:**
Find the ring road south of the city. At the roundabout for New Ross
(R700) go south for about 200 yards. The entrance for Danville House
is on your right.

This stately 1790s Georgian farmhouse situated in a peaceful location just outside Kilkenny will give you a chance to see a 100-acre dairy
farm in action. Many antiques adorn the living quarters; one bedroom
has a canopy bed (half-tester). Outside there is a large old garden with
a swing and farther back a walled kitchen garden where produce and
herbs are grown for the meals. The rooms are spacious and provide
views of the lush green farm. The dining room has a pretty chandelier over a large antique mahogany table where breakfast is served,
consisting of fresh eggs in your cooked breakfast with homemade
breads and plum, marmalade, and raspberry jams. Fishing, golfing, flying, and horseback riding can be arranged nearby. You can do all the
sights in Kilkenny while you spend your time outside in a country setting with meadows and tall mature trees. Kitty will set up the miniature
croquet set in the backyard for your amusement, or you can tour the
cowbarn at milking time, gather the eggs, and observe the inner work-
ings of an Irish farm.

Hillgrove House
Margaret and Tony Drennan
Bennetsbridge Road
Kilkenny, County Kilkenny
Telephone: 056-51453/22890
Bedrooms: 5, all with private baths.
Rates: £17 p.p.; Single £22; 50 percent discount for children under 12.
Vouchers accepted. **Credit cards:** None. **Open:** February 1 to November 30. **Children:** All ages. **Pets:** No. **Smoking:** No. **Provision for handicapped:** None. **Directions:** From Kilkenny city, take Bennetsbridge Road (R700) by the castle; the house is 2 miles down on the right, 1 mile from the roundabout.

This lovely ivy-covered house sits on a hill overlooking a patch of beautiful Irish farmland. Margaret and Tony give you a friendly welcome, and their 2 talented daughters play music and do step dancing. Margaret has a good flair for decorating—her downstairs room has small-flowered wallpaper and looks out onto the garden; the others are green and pink or peach, 2 with striped paper; some have antique wardrobes. The Drennans have a handsome Victorian living room with antiques and a TV. Their full Irish Breakfast is augmented by apple jelly and yogurt, with offerings of French toast or pancakes with maple syrup sometimes. You may also have smoked kippers or smoked trout. The dining room, at the front of the house, has a farm view. You can reach the town center easily, with its castle, museums, and abbey; or try some golf, tennis, fishing, or horseback riding very close by.

The Laurels
Teresa and Jack Nolan
College Road
Kilkenny Town, County Kilkenny
Telephone and **FAX:** 056-61501
Bedrooms: 4, all with private baths.
Rates: £17.50; 20 percent discount for children. Vouchers accepted.
Credit cards: Yes. **Open:** February to December. **Children:** Yes, 7 and
up. **Pets:** No. **Smoking:** No. **Provision for handicapped:** Yes, 1 room.
Directions: From Kilkenny Castle, turn left at lights at the intersection in town center; go up Patrick Street and turn right after Club
House Hotel. Then continue to end of road opposite Hotel Kilkenny.
Take next turning on right, turn right again, and the Laurels is on
the left.

Teresa and Jack (and their boxer dog, Cleo) are ready to welcome
you with tea and biscuits and direct you to Kilkenny's special tourist
places, many a few minutes' walk from their door. Their remodeled
home is a quiet place off the main road. The lounge looks out on the
front lawn through a large picture window. The excellent beds in the
pink, peach, and green rooms offer weary travelers a good rest. A TV
and hairdryer are provided in all rooms. Separate tables are filled in
the morning with the full Irish Breakfast, fruit and yogurts, cheese,
eggs as you like, and homemade brown bread, as well as a special pudding or potato waffles. It's a breakfast fit for a king! Nearby are championship golf courses. The Nolans are especially good at directing you
to historical and cultural features of the region.

Newlands Country House
Aileen and Seamus Kennedy
Seven Houses
Kilkenny, County Kilkenny
Telephone: 056-29111; **FAX:** 056-29171
Bedrooms: 6, all with private baths.
Rates: £20-30 p.p.; Single £20-30; 10 percent discount for children.
Vouchers not accepted. £20 elegant dinner Saturday and Wednesday
only. **Credit cards:** MasterCard, VISA. **Open:** All year, except Christmas. **Children:** Ages 12 and up. **Pets:** Only guide dogs. **Smoking:**
Restricted. **Provision for handicapped:** Yes, with help. **Directions:**
From Kilkenny, drive out Waterford Road (N10) to the roundabout.
Continue on N10 for 4 miles and turn right at Harvester Pub. The
house is ¾ miles down on the right.

Aileen and Seamus say, "Nothing is too much trouble for our
guests." They will greet you with tea in their handsome navy and pink
living room by an open fire, and you will be shown to a lovely, large
room, decorated in navy and pink or cerise. All have canopied beds,
and some have a whirlpool bath and a refrigerator. Breakfast is served
in a stunning dining room, glassed in with eight-foot windows. There
is an elaborate menu offering dishes such as plaice, kippers, lamb's
liver, hash or potato waffles, in addition to the Irish Breakfast. Outside
is another story. Seamus raises turkeys and calves for sale, but their
pets are chickens, Donks the donkey, a pony named Fred, ducks,
lambs, and Pea the peacock, who struts on top of bales of hay. You
will be close to Kilkenny Town with its golf, tennis, and crafts at the
Design Center across from the castle.

Shillogher House
Margaret and Bill Morgan
Callan Road (N76)
Kilkenny, County Kilkenny
Telephone: 056-63249/64865; **FAX:** 056-64865
Bedrooms: 5, all with private baths.
Rates: £17-18.50 p.p.; Single £25; 20 percent discount for children under 12. Vouchers accepted. **Credit cards:** VISA, Access. **Open:** All year, except December 20 to 27. **Children:** All ages. **Pets:** No. **Smoking:** No. **Provision for handicapped:** None. **Directions:** From Kilkenny City, go 1 km out the Callan Road, past the Hotel Kilkenny.

This fashionable brick house is very new and attractive. Its special feature is the glassed-in conservatory, where you may have tea and chat while enjoying the view of the gardens. The Morgans are very welcoming people, and the house has a friendly atmosphere. The rooms on 2 floors are modern with grey and pink flowers, peach and navy, or pink and wine colors. An extra bathroom with a tub is tiled in delft blue and white. The dining room is stunning and Bill does all the cooking. The large breakfast selection includes the typical Irish Breakfast, baked beans, kippers, fresh plaice, waffles with poached egg and cheese, fresh fruit, cheese board, and yogurt. They are proud of their menu. The B&B is within a few minutes of all the sights of Kilkenny and 1 hour from Cavan. Golf, fishing, and tennis are nearby.

Tir Na Nog
Mary and Eanon Wogan
Greenshill
Kilkenny, County Kilkenny
Telephone: 056-65250/62345; **FAX:** 056-63491
Bedrooms: 5, all with private baths.
Rates: £17 p.p.; Single £22; Vouchers accepted. From September 30 to March 31, Weekend Special—2 nights at £39 p.p. and dinner at a restaurant. **Credit cards:** VISA, Access, Eurocard. **Open:** All year. **Children:** Yes, 8 or older. **Pets:** No. **Smoking:** Restricted. **Provision for handicapped:** None. **Directions:** Call the hosts for directions.

Mary and Eamon Wogan work in the hotel business so you'll find some hotel-like amenities at this attractive red brick B&B. The Wogans give a hearty welcome in the large cozy lounge, and much attention to your itineraries. All 4 spacious bedrooms have TVs, hairdryers, alarm/clock radios, and a trouser press. Their colors are rose, wine and pink, and light and dark greens. The dining room has antique buffets and you may choose breakfast from a printed menu with choice of eggs in the full Irish Breakfast and even low-fat sausage. Mary bakes the bread and brews the coffee, and their eggs are farm fresh. It is only a 6- to 7-minute walk to Kilkenny Town with all its attractions, singalong pubs, castle, and museums. The Weekend Special at Tir Na Nog includes dinner at Langton's, one of the best restaurant in town with its cheery atmosphere and glass-ceiling dining room.

Carrickmourne House
Julie Doyle
New Ross Road
Thomastown, County Kilkenny
Telephone: 056-24124; **FAX:** 056-24124
Bedrooms: 5, all with private baths.
Rates: £16.50-18.50 p.p.; Single £23-25 p.p.; 20 percent discount for children under 12. Vouchers accepted. **Credit cards:** VISA, Master-Card, Eurocard. **Open:** All year, except Christmas week. **Children:** All ages. **Pets:** No. **Smoking:** Restricted. **Provision for handicapped:** None. **Directions:** From Thomastown follow the signs to Inistioge/New Ross (R700) for approximately 1 mile. The Carrickmourne House sign is on the left. Take that road up the hill for about 2 km (about 1¼ miles). The driveway is on your left.

This is a gem of a modern home surrounded by beautiful country scenery, on a woodsy hillside above the beautiful Nore Valley. Julie's husband is a custom builder and it shows. The floors are new pine, all the doors are paneled mahogany, and the spacious bedrooms are really beautifully decorated in pinks and creams, blue and creams, forest greens and rusts. The lot was selected from the Doyle family farm and trees were planted to complement the natural forest. Guests are invited to relax in the private TV lounge and browse through the local information brochures. Tea- and coffee-making facilities are in every room. The full Irish Breakfast is first rate, with fresh-squeezed orange or grapefruit juice and the care of preparation setting it apart from the usual. You can visit Jerpoint Abbey; walk, ride, or golf at the famous Mount Juliet sporting estate; or fish the Nore or Kings rivers. This is a B&B you feel like visiting more than once.

County Laois

Portlaois

N7

County Laois is bordered by Counties Kilkenny, Kildare, Offaly, and Tipperary. It is generally flatland except for the Slieve Bloom Mountains in the northwest. Just four miles east of Portlaois is the Rock of Dunmase, which was the scene of many conflicts after the invasion of the Anglo-Normans. On its summit are the ruins of a castle that was razed by Cromwell's men in 1650. We enjoyed painting watercolors here one sunny day. It is a lovely hike up to the castle ruins and a very gratifying panorama from the top of the surrounding farmlands. We saw Jersey cows grazing nearby and a small quaint Church of Ireland that is still used as a house of worship. Off the N7 going from Bally-davis north toward Portarlington is a beautiful Palladian-style mansion called Emo Court that is surrounded by beautiful gardens. Call ahead to ask when the mansion is open to the public. Drive through the Glen of O'Regan in the mountains or picnic and hike in the Monicknew Woods, south of Clonaslee. South of N7 on Swan Road is Timahoe, where there is a lovely ninety-six-foot-high Round Tower from the 1100s.

County Kildare, the horse-racing county, borders on Counties Dublin, Wicklow, Laois, and Offaly. The world-famous Curragh race-course is seven miles northwest of the large town of Naas. Other courses are at Naas and Punchestown, east of the Curragh. See and ride the finest horses of Ireland at the Frenchfurze Riding Stables east of the Curragh. Visit the Castletown House in Celbridge on the R403; social functions are still held here. The famous Japanese Gardens and National Stud Farm in Tully is a "must" visit. A good full-service restaurant, cafeteria style, is situated here. Also, there are many golf courses. Kildare Town is a beauty with Brigid's Castle and the Celtic High Cross at Noone. Fish and cruise the canals and visit Mondello Park and the Steam Museum at Straffan.

Chez-Nous
Audrey Canavan
Kilminchy
Portlaois, County Laois
Telephone: 0502-21251
Bedrooms: 5, 3 with private baths. A large suite for 4-5 people possible.
Rates: £18.50; Single £23. Vouchers accepted. **Credit cards:** None.
Open: All year, except at Christmas. **Children:** No. **Pets:** No. **Smoking:** No. **Provision for handicapped:** Restricted to walkers. **Directions:** Chez-Nous is 2 miles out from the city center on Portarlington Road, on the left as you leave the city traveling eastward. Travelers are advised to call ahead for directions as the motorway nearby is under construction.

We stayed at this lovely country home on our way from Dublin to Limerick. We enjoyed it so much we stayed two days and painted watercolors at nearby Dunamaise Castle on the Slieve Bloom Mountains. There is much to see and do in this region: golf, fishing, horseback riding, and walks. The bedrooms are beautifully decorated in cranberry and cream, pink, lavender, terra cotta, and peach and furnished with canopy beds, which adds a touch of grandeur. Rooms are named by color. The living room and hall are fashioned with fine and color-coordinated antiques. The conservatory at the rear where a sumptuous breakfast is served allows one to view the garden. The breakfast menu was impressive with the full Irish Breakfast, or fish, pancakes, and/or potato cakes. Exceptional! The table setting when we were there was a beautiful yellow and deep blue. Audrey is very clever at decorating and making you feel welcome.

ALSO RECOMMENDED: COUNTY KILDARE

Athy, *Bellindrum Farm,* Vincent and Mary Gorman, Ballindrum. Telephone: 0507-26294. Bedrooms: 3, all shared baths, all with H/C. Open April 1 to November 1. Free guided tour of this working dairy and tillage farm. Mrs. Gorman is a receptionist at the Japanese Gardens and National Stud Farm, so you can be advised as to what to see and do at this popular tourist site.

County Limerick

Limerick is a county of rolling farmlands much like Clare and is about the same size as Clare. Although Limerick is the closest large city to Shannon Airport, it's curious that it's in another county. Limerick City is old and charming with good hotels and a theater. It was a 9th-century Danish town. Take a walk across the bridge to the old castle, or peruse the many antique shops, craft shops, and art galleries. The rooftops of the city make a colorful design when seen from the train station. Visit Limerick University on the city's outskirts and see the medieval treasures in the Hunt Museum there. Visit St. Mary's Cathedral from the 12th century on Bridge Street and King John's Castle on Castle Street. The Tourist Information Office is in the old Granary on Michael Street. Bunratty Castle and Folk Park are only 10 miles northwest in County Clare.

Adare is a beautiful village about 10 miles southwest of Limerick. It has a row of shops in thatched cottages and a good selection of restaurants. Many people stay here on their first day in the Irish

Republic. Adare Manor Hotel is an elaborate Gothic building on 1,000 acres of grounds and gardens. Inside, heavy wood carvings and crystal chandeliers are a sight. Fifty of the rooms have carved fireplaces. The public may walk all around these grounds for a small fee and visit the Ogham Stone in the woods. There is a fenced-in herb garden, and we met two painters there, husband and wife, both working at their easels. About 30 miles west, over the border in County Kerry, you may want to pay a visit to Listowel, where the famous playwright John B. Keane owns and runs a pub. He lives there and is a great storyteller.

Castleview
The Glavin Family
Clonshire
Adare, County Limerick
Telephone and **FAX:** 061-396394
Bedrooms: 4; all with private baths.
Rates: £17 p.p.; Single £22; 50 percent discount for children under 12.
Vouchers accepted. £13 dinner. **Credit cards:** VISA, MasterCard/
Access, AMEX. **Open:** All year. **Children:** Yes. **Pets:** Yes. **Smoking:**
Restricted. **Provision for handicapped:** Yes, but not wheelchairs. **Directions:** From Limerick proceed to Adare on the N20 to Patrickswell,
then N21 (the Killarney Road) out of Adare. Phone the owners for
further directions.

This pretty home is well managed by Colm and Kathleen Glavin
and is in a country setting next to Clonshire Equestrian Centre.
Rooms are neat and fashionably decorated in shades of lemon, peach,
and other pastel colors. There are many amenities like tea- and coffee-
making facilities, electric blankets, hairdryers, and direct-dial telephones. Your breakfast can be ordered from an unusually tasty menu
listing main entrées such as eggs any style and bacon and sausage, or
kippers, toasted cheese, beans and toast, or hot pancakes and maple
syrup. These other items besides eggs make this a nice break from
the usual Irish cooked breakfast. The dining room is cheery and
bright with a view of the garden. We found our stay very pleasant and
comfortable. The peaceful and quiet country area makes for a nice
respite from the busy village and cities. Golf, badminton, tennis, and
walking tours are available in the charming town of Adare. Shannon
Airport is 35 minutes away.

Murphy's Cross
Pauline Bell
Adare, County Limerick
Telephone: 061-396042
Bedrooms: 5; 2 with private baths, 3 with shared.
Rates: £16 p.p. private bath; £14 p.p. shared bath; 50 percent discount for children. **Credit cards:** None. **Open:** January to December 1. **Children:** Yes. **Pets:** Yes. **Smoking:** Restricted. **Provision for handicapped:** None. **Directions:** The cottage is in Adare on Main Killarney Road, the last house on left at the *T* junction.

This 1840s cottage has the charm of an early Irish home, so it is a little different from the ordinary home. Farm animals greet you in the front yard. It used to be a thatched cottage and it has a huge 10-foot traditional Irish hearth with an old black stove in the dining room. The Bells have constructed a balcony for access to the bedrooms via steep stairs. Some bedrooms have slanted ceilings. The new one at the back is done with a pretty pine ceiling. All in all the effect is enchanting. A large bathroom with tub and shower serves the shared rooms, which have their own sink. The long table accommodates a large group for an extraordinary breakfast that includes the standard Irish cooked one (choice of eggs), but is nicely augmented by smoked kippers or fresh honeycomb yogurt. Cereals such as muesli or oatmeal (porridge), and fresh fruit in season are also available. Guests have a large cozy sitting room, with fireplace and TV, on the other side of the dining room. Adare is a quaint town you'll surely want to visit. There is a castle, an abbey, the famous Adare Manor Hotel, and numerous great restaurants in all price ranges. Mrs. Bell will advise you on these and the golfing, tennis, and antique shopping.

ALSO RECOMMENDED

Adare, *Abbey Lodge,* Mrs. Mary Dundon, Kildimo Road. Telephone: 061-396776. Bedrooms: 3, all with private baths. Credit cards accepted. Award-winning breakfasts. Cozy, comfortable home in Adare village; walk to restaurants.

Adare, *Hollywood House,* Peter and Miriam O'Shaughnessy, Croagh, situated 5 km from Adare village. Telephone: 061-396237. Bedrooms: 4, all private baths, 2 in the room or en suite. Open April 1 to November 1. Large 1690s historical farmhouse with beautifully decorated rooms. Regional award winner 1992. Beautiful setting among tall copper beeches. Tennis courts available. Charming couple.

Ballyneety, *Four Seasons,* Mrs. Mary Conway Ryan, Boherlock. Telephone: 061-351365. Bedrooms: 6 , 4 with private baths. Credit cards and vouchers accepted. Open, all year except Christmas Day. 7 km southeast of Limerick; 30 minutes to Shannon Airport. Recommended by Judy and Jerry Klinkowitz of Cedar Falls, Iowa.

Croom, *Caherass House,* Eddie O'Donnell. Telephone: 061-397053/397704. Bedrooms: 5, 4 with private baths. All major credit cards. In Croom Village take a right off N20 toward Adare; Caherass House is on right, opposite the Maigue River. Working farm bed and breakfast. Unusual hospitality. Recommended by Christian and Jody Nilsson of York, Maine.

Limerick, *Shemond House,* Raymond and Sheila Devine, Ballyglass, Clonara. Telephone: 061-34367. Bedrooms: 6, 5 with private baths. Modern family-run home. In scenic surroundings, 20 minutes from Shannon Airport and Bunratty Castle. Recommended by Mary McGinty of Ardeevin B&B, Lough Eske, Donegal Town, County Donegal.

COUNTY LOUTH

County Louth

County Louth is very small, about the same size as Dublin, and one of its features is that it borders on County Down in Northern Ireland. It also has the Irish Sea along the whole east coast. The Cooley Peninsula in the north, above Dundalk, is a very special sight to see. Begin at Ballymascanlon, take R173, and do a loop around the point of land, stopping at the quaint village of Gyles Quay, and a little farther, King John's Castle. Some of the green sheep-covered hills in the countryside there remind us of scenes in Dingle.

Dundalk is the largest city in Louth. It is a port and has history back to A.D. 600, and has churches and cathedrals to visit. The salt marshes east of the city are home to one of Ireland's best bird sanctuaries and you may spot some very unusual species there. North of town, visit the very curious rounded Neolithic mound called Proleek Dolmen, dating to 3000 B.C.

Industrial Drogheda, surrounded by farms, in the south on the Boyne River, claims a large corner of the famous Battle of the Boyne site. This very historical Viking town dates back to A.D. 911. It was once entirely walled in, and you may still view parts of the wall and the lovely medieval St. Laurence's Gate. Visit Monasterboice with 10th-century High Crosses, and Mellifont Abbey near the Meath border. In the north of Louth, you can drive to Iniskeen in Monaghan, and in the south, you can drive over to see the famed stony tombs at Newgrange in County Meath.

Highfield House Farm
Kitty and Jim McEvoy
Termonfeckin
Drogheda, County Louth
Telephone: 041-22172
Bedrooms: 3, all with private baths.
Rates: £17 p.p.; 50 percent discount for children under 12. Vouchers not accepted. **Credit cards:** None. **Open:** March 1 to October 31. **Children:** All ages. **Pets:** No. **Smoking:** Restricted to lounge. **Provision for handicapped:** None. **Directions:** From Drogheda town, take R166 to Termonfeckin, 5 miles northeast. Go down in a vale and over a humpy bridge, and just on the left see the pub and Triple House Restaurant. Highfield House Farm is just past it on the left at the corner, a 2-story stucco with a stone wall and white gate.

This lovely 1725 farmhouse has been in the McEvoy family since 1928. Termonfeckin is in a quaint and picturesque section of Drogheda, while the town center is rather dowdy. Kitty and Jim may greet you in the farmyard; then you will get a cup of tea. We had ours in the wonderful antique kitchen. The house has a handsome big entryway and the rooms are all large and nostalgic, with antique beds and flowered covers in soft colors of lilac, peach and cream, and yellow. The dining room has a fireplace and a large hand-carved rosewood sideboard. The huge lounge has a TV and antique furniture, featuring lovely matching Victorian "fainting chairs." Kitty was given an award by Bord Fáilte for Best Breakfast in the county. Her full Irish Breakfast includes homemade brown bread with raisins, fresh eggs from their own red hens, fruit, and white or black pudding. Ask about the secret room and the tunnels in the fields; Jim loves to tell the history of the house and town. Livestock, grain, turkeys, and goats are raised on the farm. One mile from the Irish Sea and a sandy beach, this is a good place to visit the Battle of the Boyne artifacts, the Druid site at Newgrange, 2 18-hole golf courses, pubs, and castles of Drogheda.

Tullyesker Country House
Cepta McDonnell
Monasterboice
Drogheda, County Louth
Telephone: 041-30430; **FAX:** 041-32624
Bedrooms: 5, all with private baths.
Rates: £19 p.p. to £23 p.p. for a double room. Vouchers not accepted.
Credit cards: None. **Open:** March 1 to October 31. **Children:** Yes, 7
or older. **Pets:** No. **Smoking:** Restricted. **Provision for handicapped:**
None. **Directions:** From Drogheda, take N1 north. The B&B is 3 miles
north of Drogheda on N1 at Tullyesker Hill. The house is on the right-
hand side surrounded by trees.

This marvelous getaway B&B is nested on Tullyesker Hill amid four
acres of gardens with panoramic views of the Boyne Valley. Cepta
McDonnell's luxurious jewel-toned rooms are lavishly appointed with
electric blankets, TVs, hairdryers, toiletries, and tea- and coffee-making facilities. The breakfast menu has more items to choose from than
any other we've seen in Ireland. It includes such unusual items as a
cheese platter with savory biscuits, poached smoked herring with
lemon and grilled tomato, Irish smoked salmon and eggs, chicken
liver pâté, and what they call a "symphony of fruit," a Tullyesker
favorite. Besides these and many different types of eggs, porridge,
cereal, and yogurt, there are homemade scones and bread, Bewley's
tea and coffee (including decaf!), and Cadbury's hot chocolate. There
are tennis courts and walks on the property in the gardens or the
woodland. Within driving distance is the 17-foot-high Monasterboice
Cross, which has many figures and ornamental designs carved in
stone. And just over the border in Meath are the Mellifont Abbey,
famous Boyne Valley, Hill of Stone, and fascinating burial mound at
Newgrange. The ocean is only a few miles to the east.

COUNTY MAYO

County Mayo

Mayo is another very large county with 2 lakes, Lough Conn and Lough Mask. From Sligo, you may want to take the R313 out to the Mullet Peninsula to the northwest to explore the unspoiled rolling farmlands with sheep and cattle, and its bogs. There is good fishing on the rocks and from the shore at most coastal areas. The town between 2 bays, Belmullet, is quite fancy and modernized. Enjoy the views of sweeping, multicolored grasses of the bogs, and the mystical view of Benwee Head with its stark profile. Farther south you may drive out R319 directly to Achill Island for a look at high cliffs and sandy beaches, and there are pubs with music, too.

You may cut down to the classy town of Westport. It has a nice town center with lots of shops, galleries, cafés, and pubs, and it is very proud of its Sailing Centre. There are some breathtaking views of Clew Bay and Croagh Patrick Mountain, with the huge white statue of St. Patrick standing watch at the top. Here St. Patrick made a 40-day fast, and in honor of him, modern-day pilgrims climb this mountain on the last Sunday of each July.

Throughout Mayo there are a good deal of antique and craft shops. Cong, on the southern border, has the ruins of the Royal Abbey of Cong, Ashford Castle, and it was the town where most of *Quiet Man* was filmed. Knock, a town in the eastern section of Mayo, is known for its Marian Shrine, where an apparition of Our Lady was seen in 1879 at the church of St. John the Baptist. Thousands of pilgrims visit this each year.

Devard
Nora Ward
Westport Road
Castlebar, County Mayo
Telephone: 094-23462
Bedrooms: 4; 3 with private bath (en suite), 1 with separate.
Rates: £16 p.p.; Single £21; 50 percent discount for children. Vouchers accepted. **Credit cards:** None. **Open:** March 1 to November 30.
Children: All ages. **Pets:** Outside. **Smoking:** Yes. **Provision for handicapped:** Yes, first floor ramp. **Directions:** Devard is on Westport Road (the N60), 1 km outside town on the left just after Spar convenience store.

This is a really comfortable modern bungalow with nicely decorated rooms and a very pleasant hostess in Nora Ward. All the bedrooms are fitted with TV, tea- and coffee-making facilities, and electric blankets, and matching bedspreads and curtains, and are spacious by Irish standards. They are done in burgundies, brown and blue with cocoa rugs, and peach with white and cream duvets. The baths are also large with bidet, shower, toilet, tiles to the ceiling in pretty coordinated colors, gold fixtures, and parquet floors. Devard is set apart from the usual in style and decor. One room has a beautiful view of the rose garden. Breakfast is the full Irish cooked breakfast, supplemented with white and black puddings, French toast, porridge, yogurt, fruit, etc. But the brewed coffee hit the spot after drinking so much instant for breakfast. We are spoiled; we like ours fresh brewed as we had in our own B&B. There is a handsome marble fireplace in the combination sitting and dining room. But to us the gracious and genuinely warm Nora Ward made this home special. This is a good place to stop while traveling south to Westport from Ballina or Sligo Town. Check out the Breaffy House Hotel for an evening meal.

Carrabaun House
Angela Gavin
Carrabaun
Westport, County Mayo
Telephone: 098-26196
Bedrooms: 5, all with private baths.
Rates: £17 p.p.; Single £22; 25 percent discount for children under 10.
Credit cards: Yes. **Open:** March 1 to December 10. **Children:** All ages.
Pets: No. **Smoking:** Restricted. **Provision for handicapped:** Yes. **Directions:** From Castlebar, you enter on Castlebar Street. Go over the bridge, up Bridge Street, and turn right at the clock. Cross over Shop Street and continue on to Monmument Street. Take a left up Peter Street and continue on Tubber Hill Road. At the back of the hill, turn left on N59 after the railway bridge. After Maxol gas station, look for the Carrabaun House sign on the left. Enter the driveway through the large white pillars.

This neo-Georgian home, with panoramic views of Croagh Patrick, Clew Bay, Clare Island, and the rolling green fields and stone walls, sits atop a hill just outside Westport so you have the peace and quiet of a country setting, yet all the many tourist features of Westport close at hand. We found the entryway and ascending staircase of regal proportions. The equally spacious rooms are all very new and colorfully decorated in lime greens, pinks and reds, and one in periwinkle blue with a delft-blue duvet. All have beautiful matching drapes and white dressing tables. You get a bright and fresh feeling. A bay window has been added to the guest lounge on the first floor. Ask the Gavins to point out the best walks, golfing, bowling, fishing spots, and other recreational features of Westport. But come morning they will stuff you full of a tasty Irish Breakfast plus choices of puddings, cheeses, fruit, yogurts, etc.

Coral Reef
Anne Colgan
Lecanvey
Westport, County Mayo
Telephone: 098-64814
Bedrooms: 5; 3 with private baths, 2 with shared.
Rates: £14 p.p.; Single £16; Vouchers accepted. £11 dinner. **Credit cards:** None. **Open:** April to October 31. **Children:** Yes. **Pets:** No. **Smoking:** Yes. **Provision for handicapped:** None. **Directions:** Take R335 and wind your way along the coast west of Westport on Louisburgh Road for 8 miles. The Coral Reef is on your left facing the sea.

The seashore of Clew Bay is across the road and the majestic Croagh Patrick is behind, where pilgrims make their barefooted climb in July. The Coral Reef is a lovely place to get close to the water and daydream. This is a modern, large bungalow with rooms on the main floor and 2 more rooms and a separate guest lounge with a TV upstairs, which is reached by a spiral staircase. Various accommodations from twins to king-sized beds and a family room are available. We especially liked the room with a view of Achill Island. Anne Colgan is a talented cook and offers a wonderful evening meal by prior arrangement. But her breakfast menu can also stand on its own merits. There is the standard Irish Breakfast but it is augmented by wonderful hot baked breads and scones just out of the oven, French toast, pancakes, and syrup. It is just what you need before you go fishing, surfing, sailing, golfing, or just beachcombing along the bay. Have Anne tell you the story of Croagh Patrick and where it got its name.

ALSO RECOMMENDED

Castlebar, *Lakeview House,* Mary Moran, Westport Road. Telephone: 094-22374. Bedrooms: 4, all with private baths. Vouchers accepted. Nice place. Mary has been offering her reliable and pleasant hospitality for since 1972. South from Castlebar on the Westport Road (N60), about 4 miles on left.

Charlestown, *Hawthorne House,* Mrs. Josephine Keane, N5. Telephone: 094-54237. Bedrooms: 5, all with shared baths. Lovely and elegantly furnished period house. Charming and courteous innkeeper.

Westport, *Fair Lawns,* Mrs. Sheila Ree, Lecanvey. Telephone: 098-64950. Bedrooms: 4, all with private baths. Vouchers accepted. £11 dinner. Noted for excellent hospitality and cuisine. Recommended by Maeve Walsh of Tubbercurry, County Sligo.

Westport, *Glenderan,* Dermot and Ann O'Flaherty, Rosbeg. Telephone: 098-26585. Bedrooms: 3, 2 with private baths. 1 km outside Westport 600 m off Louisburgh Road.

COUNTY MEATH

County Meath

Although County Meath borders on County Dublin, the people are as far from the worldly urban style of Dubliners as Irishmen can be. The mystical spirits of the ancients prevail. In this country made up strictly of farms and small towns, history in the form of Bronze-Age tombs and burial mounds swirls about. The Hill of Tara, where most believe the High Kings of Ireland reigned in the 11th century, is just south of Navan. Newgrange, a circular tomb made of stones probably about 1500 B.C., is preserved in excellent condition. A large rock positioned at its opening only allows a thin stream of light inside on December 21 each year for 17 minutes. There are curious markings on some of the stones inside. It's quite an experience to stand inside with a guide, with artificial light and other visitors, and ponder its vast age. Newgrange has smaller lines waiting to get in in September and October. In order to get in on December 21, you must put your name on a list that's backed up a few years. They only escort about 10 to 14 in at a time. Even in summer, you should take a look from outside. The mounds of Nowth and Dowth nearby are worth a visit, too.

There are also more Boyne battlefields to visit in the area. Kids of all ages will enjoy the working Newgrange Farm in Slane, where they can touch every kind of soft farm animal imaginable. There are castles, too, at Trim and south of Navan.

A visit to the town of Kells will round out your magical tour. This is where Scottish monks in the 9th century, in St. Columba's Monastery, wrote, illustrated, and preserved *The Book of Kells,* a Latin interpretation of the four Gospels. A copy of it can be seen in St. Columba's Church of Ireland there in Kells. The original, of course, can be viewed at Trinity College in Dublin.

Roughgrange Farm
Irene McDonnell
Donore
Drogheda, County Meath
Telephone: 041-23147
Bedrooms: 4, all with private baths.
Rates: £17 p.p. Vouchers accepted. **Credit cards:** VISA. **Open:** February to November. **Children:** All ages. **Pets:** No. **Smoking:** No. **Provision for handicapped:** None. **Directions:** From Drogheda take Donore Village Road on the south side of Boyne River. In Donore Village, go right toward Dublin Road (N2). Roughgrange is on your left.

This beautiful 17th-century farmhouse B&B is situated in the most historic of valleys in Ireland. It is overlooking the scenic Boyne Valley and is 1.5 km from Newgrange, Nowth, and Dowth. The large living and dining rooms are furnished with handsome period antiques and with fireplaces to provide warmth and coziness. A full, sumptuous country breakfast is served on a large antique table. Homemade scones, brown bread, black and white pudding, tomato, plus traditional breakfast will get you off to a good start as you visit some of Ireland's most cherished treasures of antiquity—the Hill of Tara, Mellifont Abbey, Monasterboice Crosses, Newgrange, or Kells. Newgrange is the most impressive pre-Celtic tomb. Salmon, trout, and coarse fishing on 280 acres is free to guests. If you like pastoral scenery with sheep and cattle, this is the place for you. If you have any energy left over, golf, swimming, and tennis are within easy reach. The McDonnells will greet you with a warm welcome and advise you of the way to get the most out of your visit to Meath.

Boyne Dale
Paula Casserly
Donaghmore, Slane Road
Navan, County Meath
Telephone: 046-28015
Bedrooms: 3, all with private baths.
Rates: £16 p.p. private bath; Single £21; 20 percent discount for children under 12. Vouchers accepted. **Credit cards:** None. **Open:** April 1 to October 31. **Children:** Up to age 12. **Pets:** None. **Smoking:** No. **Provision for handicapped:** No. **Directions:** The house is 2.4 km east of Navan town on the Slane Road (the N51).

This modern bungalow is in the countryside of the famed Boyne Valley, site of the historical Battle of the Boyne. Paula Casserly is bright, enjoyable, and very organized. The rooms—orange, blues and cream, and pink—are pretty with wide windows overlooking gardens. The handsome dining room has a fireplace, separate tables, and a large window with a view. Choose your breakfast from a menu. It is typical Irish with a choice of beans or cheese; ask ahead for yogurt. Horseback riding is ½ mile away. An 18-hole golf course, public swimming pools, snooker, a racecourse, and movies are all nearby. Visit the Dunmore Castle, and September is the best time to see Newgrange and the Round Tower, 10 minutes away.

ALSO RECOMMENDED

Ashbourne, *Aisling,* Evelyn and Seamus Daly, Baltransa, on Dublin/ Derry Road (N2). Telephone: 01-350359/351135. Bedrooms: 9, 6 with private baths. Vouchers accepted. Modern home, 2 km outside Ashbourne. Ideal for Dublin Airport 17 km away. Recommended by Josephine Martin of Mount Royd country home, Carrigans, County Donegal.

Navan, *Gainstown House,* Mrs. Mary Reilly, Trim Road (2 miles south of Navan). Telephone: 046-21448. Bedrooms: 4, 1 private bath, but H/C in room. Vouchers accepted. Spacious period farm residence, pleasantly decorated, on 200 acres. Fishing, golf, swimming, and horseback riding available locally.

Slane, *Conyngham Arms Hotel,* Mr. Kevin MacKen. Telephone: 041-24155; FAX: 041-24205. Book in U.S. on 800-223-1588, Canada 800-531-6767. Bedrooms: 16. A village inn on main road. The deluxe bedrooms are beautiful. A good bargain for inn accommodations.

Slane, *Hillview,* Mrs. Lily Bagnall, Gernonstown. Telephone: 041-24327. Bedrooms: 5, 3 with private baths. Vouchers accepted. Just a mile west of Slane center off N51, take road on right. Modern home looking out on beautiful Boyne Valley. Well decorated. Very clean and neat.

County Monaghan

On entering quiet County Monaghan, you note that there are fewer cars, although the road is wider and the countryside stretches out in wide sweeps of farms. In Carrickmacross you'll find traditional lace, which you can buy at the Carrickmacross Lace Coop. Inishkeen is the birthplace of the celebrated Irish poet Patrick Kavanagh. Monaghan is a good-sized town of fishing fame, is also known for its County Museum, which was an old market house in 1792. Andy's Restaurant in the center of town has good food and service, reasonable prices, and lots of class. We stopped there for lunch and were very impressed. Rossmore Forest Park with its beautiful nature walks and lakes is just to the south of Monaghan Town. The town of Clones to the southwest is noted for its Augustinian Abbey of the 12th century with its 75-foot Round Tower, a 10th-century Celtic carved cross in the town center, and the Clones Lace Centre, where you can buy the lace of the ancient craft passed down through the centuries.

The Cedars
Mary McArdle
Clones Road
Monaghan, County Monaghan
Telephone: 047-82783
Bedrooms: 3; 2 with private baths, 1 with shower in room, toilet in hall.
Rates: £16.50 p.p.; Single £21.50; 50 percent discount for children
under 12. Vouchers accepted. **Credit cards:** None. **Open:** January 8
to December 18. **Children:** All ages. **Pets:** Yes. **Smoking:** No. **Provision for handicapped:** None. **Directions:** From Monaghan Town, take
Clones Road (N54, A3); the house is on a hill at the end of a row of
houses on the right, about ½ mile. You'll see a shamrock and a large
sign for Agrihealth Company at the foot of the driveway shared by The
Cedars.

This modern, stone-front, split-level home on a hillside has great
views of the town of Monaghan and the rolling hills or "drumlins" of
the countryside. It was recommended to us by the owner of Andy's
Restaurant in the town center. The bedrooms are attractive, clean, and
neat and guests have a private entry at the side door. The living room
has a comfortable settee and chairs, TV, and tea-making facilities.
The dining room has a balcony and huge sliding glass doors for a
grand view of the hills. Besides the typical Irish Breakfast, Mary offers
freshly squeezed orange juice, grapefruit segments and prunes, several cereals including porridge, and percolated coffee. Recreational
features of the area are walking in Forest Park or Beagan Mountains,
fishing, 18-hole golf, horseback riding, and a swimming pool.

Willow Bridge Lodge
Ann Holden
Silver Stream
Armagh Road
Monaghan Town, County Monaghan
Telephone and **FAX:** 47-81054; e-mail: motelbandb@tinet.ie
Bedrooms: 5, all with private baths; 2 motel-style suites with full facilities.
Rates: £22.50 p.p.; Single £25; discount for children. Vouchers not
accepted. **Credit cards:** None. **Open:** January 4 to December 20. **Children:** Yes, all ages. **Pets:** No. **Smoking:** No. **Provision for handicapped:**
None. **Directions:** Take Armagh road (N12) out of Monaghan Town.
Pass army camp on left, a straight stretch of 500 yards. At the Willow
Bridge Lodge sign, turn left, go down the driveway and over a small
bridge; the large bungalow to the left on top of the hill is Willow
Bridge.

This a handsome and spacious motel-style bed and breakfast is set
in a beautiful garden with panoramic views. The interior has a creative
blend of red and blue colors and natural wood paneling. All rooms
are furnished with king-sized beds, beautiful natural wood floors, en
suite baths, TVs with satellite and movie channels, hairdryers, and
tea- and coffee-making facilities. There is an inside spacious and
attractive lounge for conversing with other guests that is furnished
with a large TV and comfortable leatherette chairs and sofas. You will
also find an outside patio where you can enjoy nature and the fresh
air. Monaghan is the crossroads of Ireland, the main crossing point for
ancient Irish kings, where they crisscrossed to do battle. But today
you can break your journey for a peaceful and warm welcome by Bill
and Ann Holden. A full Irish Breakfast is served.

COUNTY OFFALY

County Offaly

Bordered by Westmeath on the north, Kildare on the east, Laois and Tipperary on the south, and the River Shannon and Galway on the west, Offaly is centrally located in Ireland but it is not far from Dublin. Visit the Birr Castle with its surrounding gardens and one hundred-acre demesne. It was originally a fort that bore the hallmark of the Normans, Cromwellians, Jacobites, and Williamites and survived numerous sieges. See the ruins of Clonmacnoise on the left bank of the Shannon, one of the most extensive monastic sites in Ireland including a cathedral, two roundhouses, churches, castle, and Celtic crosses. St. Ciaran founded a monastery here in A.D. 545. This settlement derives much of its beauty from being on the Shannon. The Irish Mist factory can be visited in Tullamore and the Grand Canal passing through here offers visitors an opportunity for boating and bird watching. Banagher on the Shannon also offers cruises from its marina, an excellent place to hire a pleasure cruiser. The Slieve Bloom Mountains and the Shannon give Offaly its special character.

Canal View Country House
Bernadette Keyes
Killina Road
Rahan
Tullamore, County Offaly
Telephone: 0506-55868; **FAX:** 0506-55825
Bedrooms: 4; 3 with private baths, 1 with shared.
Rates: Double £17 p.p.; Single £22; 33 percent discount for children. Vouchers accepted. £15 dinner. **Credit cards:** all except American Express. **Open:** All year. **Children:** All ages. **Pets:** No. **Smoking:** Restricted. **Provision for handicapped:** None. **Directions:** From center of Tullamore, take Birr Road (N52) for 2 miles out. Go through Mullagh Village with a church, then take the next right. You will see the sign here for Canal View. Go 2½ miles to the third bed and breakfast on the right.

Situated on the banks of the Grand Canal, this modern, lovely home is also a leisure center. Bernadette is very generous and efficient in the way she runs her business, which includes paddleboats and rowboats at no charge for guests. She also has a new sauna and steam bathroom, as well as a whirlpool for guests. Her rooms are attractive and comfortable. One room is pink with roses, another is gold and brown, and there is one family room decorated with blue and pink flowers. She serves a full Irish Breakfast plus fresh fruit, yogurt, porridge, and potato waffles. Along with fishing on the canal, you can enjoy golf, horseback riding, walking trails, and a guided tour to show the wildlife of the bogs and eskers. Irish music is played at local pubs, and a cinema, dancing, and bingo can be found in Tullamore.

County Roscommon

County Roscommon is in the heart of Ireland and is mostly flat plain, making it great farm country. There are just enough boglands, meadows, and low rolling hills dotted with lakes to make it very pleasant to visit. In the north you'll find Lough Key Forest Park, 840 acres with trails for hiking and boats on the lake for renting. There are bog gardens with heather and other small plants to study. Eat at the Lakeshore Restaurant with picture windows overlooking the water. Very nearby is the town of Boyle, situated between 2 lakes, with the fascinating

13th-century Boyle Abbey all in its ancient splendor. This town and surrounding area is a paradise for walkers and fishermen.

The famous blind harpist Turlough O'Carolan (died 1738), is buried at Kilronan Abbey Cemetery, 4 miles northeast of Lough Key. At Castlerea, farther south, is the Clonalis House, built in the 1800s, home of the chieftan of the O'Conor Clan. Here you may view O'Carolan's harp, old glassware, paintings, and Gaelic manuscripts. Afternoon tea is served.

In the center of the county is the historical capitol, Roscommon, a large town where sheep and cattle raising are the main occupations. Visit the Norman stronghold of Roscommon Castle and the ruins of Roscommon Abbey with its 8 sculptures representing medieval Irish soldiers. Northeast of Roscommon city is Strokestown with its Gothic arch leading to Strokestown Park House, built in 1660, a captivating place to visit. This town is also the home of Slieve Baun Handcrafts, sold in the markets and shops all over town.

Abbey House
Christina and Martin Mitchell
Boyle, County Roscommon
Telephone: 079-62385
Bedrooms: 6; 5 with private baths, 1 with shared.
Rates: £17 p.p. private bath; £15 p.p. shared bath; Single £19-22.50; discounts for children; £160 per week for self-catering cottages. Vouchers accepted. **Credit cards:** None. **Open:** March 1 to November 1. **Children:** All ages. **Pets:** No. **Smoking:** Yes. **Provision for handicapped:** None. **Directions:** Take N4, Dublin/Sligo Road, to Boyle; the house is ½ km away from town center on the grounds of Boyle Abbey.

This Georgian house covered with ivy, on lovely grounds between the Abbey and a river, is a delight. Martin and Christina work hard at giving guests good personal service and help with touring. You may want to wander through the gardens or walk to the Forest Park, not far away. All rooms are pleasant and the lounge has a TV and an open fire. The Mitchells serve a typical full Irish Breakfast. The house is 110 miles from Dublin, midway between there and Donegal. Boyle is only 20 miles from the famous town of Sligo. Walk 4 minutes to town, try one of the two 9-hole golf courses locally, or fish the many lakes and rivers of the beautiful surrounding area. The pleasant hosts will give you all sorts of hints on where to go.

COUNTY SLIGO

County Sligo

County Sligo is a patchwork of rugged mountains, rolling hills, and sparkling lakes and rivers. The many coves and bays have splendid beaches to enjoy. Starting in the north, coming out of Donegal, you'll reach the wonderful Yeats country right away. You'll see the undulating, moss-green Ben Bulben Mountain and the church spire at Drumcliffe, where W. B. Yeats' father was a minister and where Yeats is buried. The high Celtic cross that he mentions in a poem is here. He called Sligo the "Land of Heart's Desire." Rosses Point and Strandhill are beautiful beaches and the way the sea comes up, you can view mountains, sea, and Drumcliffe all at once. You will be able to visit 60 megalithic mounds and tombs built by Stone-Age man in Carrowmore, outside Sligo Town, and in other places in the county. Sligo is a colorful old town with history, good restaurants, art galleries, music, and theater. The Hawk's Well Theatre on Temple Street has good entertainment year round. Lissadell House and Gardens, built in the 1830s, was the home of the famous Gore-Booth family. The Yeats Memorial Building on High Bridge is a must-see attraction. There is also a Yeats signposted country tour of Sligo beauty spots.

Driving south to Tubbercurry, you'll see the breathtaking Ox Mountains and panoramic Ladies Brae. Tubbercurry is the home of the South Sligo Summer School of Traditional Irish Music and Dance, held every July, where you can learn something about playing the fiddle, pennywhistle, bodhran drums, Uillean pipes, and set and step dancing. If you wish to participate, please contact Rita Flannery, Tubbercurry, County Sligo, Ireland, or call her at 071-85010. Don't forget to visit Killoran's Restaurant, which has an Irish party every Thursday night from June to September. Everyone gets a chance to churn the butter, taste the "boxty" potato cakes and hot scones, and sing and dance all night.

Sligo County is a great place for horseback riding (ponytrekking), golfing, fishing, cycling, and every water sport you can imagine. You can easily visit Donegal and Leitrim to the north, and County Mayo to the south with its beautiful Westport and the Croagh Patrick Mountain.

Silver Seas
Teresa Noone
Cregg
Rosses Point, County Sligo
Telephone: 071-45997
Bedrooms: 5; 3 with private baths, 2 with shared.
Rates: £17 p.p. private bath; £15 p.p. shared bath; Single £18; 25 percent discount for children under 12. Vouchers accepted. **Credit cards:** All major ones. **Open:** March 1 to November 30. **Children:** All ages. **Pets:** No. **Smoking:** Yes. **Provision for handicapped:** Yes. **Directions:** Off the N15, take Rosses Point Road for 3 miles, turn right at Cregg House, turn right again, and the house is on your left.

This beautiful home near Rosses Point Beach is a great discovery. The panoramic views on all sides are pastoral and lovely—farms and sea and the Ben Bulben Mountain. Teresa, the courteous hostess, serves tea and loves to show you around her attractive modern home. The large living room with sliding glass doors faces the bay. The couches are soft, deep, and inviting. Harry, the border collie, may wag you a hello. One bedroom has knotty pine panelling and floral matching designs. The colors of the rooms are pink and blue, green, and lavender—all are very pretty and roomy. Some face Sligo Bay and some, Drumcliffe Bay and Mountains. Teresa's very proud of her bright, oversized, raspberry-tiled bath, with tub, bidet, and shower, the shared bath for 2 rooms. Breakfast in the sunny dining room is typical full Irish with offers of cereals, fruit, yogurt, and cheeses for variety. This house is close to 2 beaches; Rosses Point is safer for children. Yeats' grave, Drumcliffe church and mountains, golf, horseback riding, and Sligo Town are all very nearby.

Aisling

Des and Nan Faul
Cairns Hill
Sligo, County Sligo
Telephone: 071-60704
Bedrooms: 5; 3 with private baths, 2 with shared.
Rates: £18 p.p. private bath; £16 p.p. shared bath; Single £5 extra.
Vouchers accepted. **Credit cards:** None. **Open:** All year, except
December 21-28. **Children:** No. **Pets:** No. **Smoking:** No. **Provision for
handicapped:** None. **Directions:** From Dublin-Galway: On N4, turn
right at first set of traffic lights onto Cairns Road. From Donegal, get
on N4 and turn left at the traffic lights after the Esso Station. Aisling
is the second bed and breakfast on the left.

The Fauls have a modern bungalow in a peaceful, scenic location
overlooking Sligo Bay in Yeats country. It is a comfortable family home
surrounded by large gardens. The five rooms are decorated in pastel
blues, pinks, and creams, and all have TVs, hairdryers, and electric
blankets. The dining room has a beautiful view of Sligo Bay and the
imposing, rolling, green Ben Bulben Mountain. Nan serves yogurt
and fruit in addition to her full Irish Breakfast. You may visit any of the
several beautiful beaches nearby or walk 20 minutes to Sligo Town.
There are golf courses, horseback riding, and cinemas nearby. It's
just a short ride to the church and the huge Celtic cross near Yeats'
grave. Visit the Sports Complex in Sligo, too.

Lissadell
Mary Cadden
Pearse Road
Sligo, County Sligo
Telephone: 071-61937
Bedrooms: 4, all with private baths.
Rates: £17 p.p.; Single £22; Vouchers not accepted. **Credit cards:** None. **Open:** All year, except few days at Christmas. **Children:** Yes, 12 or older. **Pets:** No. **Smoking:** No. **Provision for handicapped:** None.
Directions: From Sligo Town, turn left onto Dublin Road N4, and at the Silver Swan Hotel turn right. The 2-story house is on the right; look for the red door.

This ivy-covered white stucco house is from the 1910s and very close to Sligo Town. Mary, a pleasant hostess, greets you with tea and scones and will show you her attractive, neat, and spacious rooms, decorated with ruffled pillows in pastel flowers of pink or peach and white. Her lounge is very comfy with a TV and her stately dining room has one long antique table. All is very trim and neat. Besides her full Irish Breakfast, you may choose a continental breakfast of cereal and scones. You may walk to town or ride a few minutes to Strandhill or Rosses Point beaches. Visit Lough Gill with boat rides, or the Drumcliffe Mountains and Yeats country just 10 minutes away. Horseback riding is available just 20 minutes away in the country town of Carrowmore, where you may also see the megalithic burial mounds.

Stonecroft
Mary Conway
Off Donegal Road N15
Kintogher
Sligo, County Sligo
Telephone: 071-45667
Bedrooms: 4, all with private baths.
Rates: £17 p.p. private bath; £16.50 p.p. shared bath; Single £19.50-21;
20 percent discount for children under 12. Vouchers accepted. **Credit cards:** VISA, MasterCard, and AMEX. **Open:** March 1 to December 8.
Children: 2 years and older. **Pets:** No. **Smoking:** Restricted. **Provision for handicapped:** Yes. **Directions:** Stonecroft is 3 miles north of Sligo Town off Donegal Road N15 on the left side.

Mary Conway, a warm, generous hostess, welcomes you with tea or coffee in her peaceful, spacious home. Her living room and 2 of the guest rooms look out over farmlands to the majestic Ben Bulben Mountain, soft, folded, and moss green like the Pali in Hawaii. The famous Drumcliffe church spire can be seen across the road, and over a large sweep of land to the left you can view the beautiful Drumcliffe Bay. Mary will spend time with you, mapping out routes for touring the area, full of history, where Yeats lived and was buried. The rooms, all on the first floor, are attractive with TV and tea- and coffee-making facilities. The matching drapes and quilts are of an unusual modern design in orange and grey or pale green and mulberry. At night, you may eat in the Yeats Tavern, watch TV, and visit with her younger boys, David and Mark, as we did. Breakfast is the typical Irish with added fruited yogurt, fresh fruit, and tantalizing hot, crunchy scones. Rosses Point Beach, golf, country walks, Lough Gill boat trips, surfing, and theater are nearby.

ALSO RECOMMENDED

Sligo/Duncliff, *Rathnashee,* Tess and Sean Haughey, Teesan, Donegal Road. Telephone: 071-43376. Bedrooms: 4, 2 with private baths. Open all year. Scenic location 2 miles from Sligo town center on N15. Very hospitable hosts who can provide information on archeological tours in the region.

Sligo Town, *Tree Tops,* Ronan and Doreen MacEvilly, Cleveragh Road. Telephone: 071-60160/62301. Bedrooms: 5, 4 with private baths. Large and nicely decorated bedrooms. Secluded, lovely home. 5-minute walk to town center.

County Tipperary

A drive southeast from Limerick Town will take you across rich farmlands through Pallasgreen with its excellent Chaser O'Brien pub/
restaurant, on to Tipperary Town, a farming center, then to the quaint
town of Bansha in a vale that is surrounded by beautiful hills. We liked
this little village and spent some time here. There is an Equestrian
Center at the beautiful Bansha House, where racehorses are trained,

and where one can experience a wonderful horseback ride through the countryside. One should allow time to take the beautiful drive up the Glen of Aherlow, cross over the mountain on the R662, where there is a lookout with a large Christ statue, and turn right on the I119 to Tipperary Town. South of Bansha is the town of Cahir with the beautifully restored, 15th-century Cahir Castle, where tours are available. To the southeast there are the scenic drives to the market towns of Clonmel and Carrick on Suir, sited in an extremely picturesque region. Stop at Kinsell's pub for a pint and a snack, just outside the West Gate of Clonmel when you make your southern swing through Tipperary.

Make sure you visit the famous Rock of Cashel, a steep outcrop of limestone, once a fortress where ancient chieftains were crowned and that later became a Gothic cathedral in the 13th century with side chapels. Allow time to have a leisurely visit with a snack and tea at one of the quaint shops near the parking lot before you hike up the road to tour the castle. The area around Cashel is quite pretty and is worthy of an overnight stay. Local shops have the famous Shanagarry tweeds. The Cashel Palace Hotel, a Queen Anne-style building, was once the residence of the archbishops of the Church of Ireland.

Other features of Tipperary are the Kilcooley Abbey, the Abbey of the Holy Cross, and the attractive church at Fethard. Remember the two-day rule. Try to locate a bed and breakfast as a base camp, make side trips from there, and return to your host family in the evening. It's more fun that way.

Dualla House
Martin Mairead and Robert Power
Dualla/Kilkenny Road
Cashel, County Tipperary
Telephone and **FAX:** 062-61487
Bedrooms: 4, all with private baths.
Rates: £20 p.p. private bath; £15 p.p. shared bath; 33½ percent discount for children. Vouchers accepted. **Credit cards:** None. **Open:** March 1 to December 1. **Children:** All ages. **Pets:** Yes. **Smoking:** No. **Provision for handicapped:** None. **Directions:** On R691, signposted near church, travel 4 km from Cashel on the Dualla/Killkenney Road. The Dualla House is 1 km from Dualla Village. House is on the left with a sign at the gate.

The Dualla House farm and B&B is set in the scenic countryside in the Golden Vale of Tipperary. A Georgian house, it was built in the 1790s by Rody Scully, a local landlord. Going uphill through the entry driveway, you'll see fields fulll of sheep on either side. Martin Mairead and Robert Power have more than 1,000 ewes, and they breed Suffolk Crosses and Cheviot Crosses. Their rams are mainly Suffolk and North Country. The guest rooms have flowered walls with matching bedcovers, antique beds and furniture, and lovely prints of country scenes on the walls. All have tea-making facilities and grand views of sheep fields. Mairead's delectable breakfasts are comprised of a choice of traditional eggs, sausages, and hams with homemade breads and preserves, a choice of cereals or porridge, fresh fruit, yogurt, and juices. On the property there are farm walks and their colorful, neatly laid-out gardens to enjoy. Nearby you will find tennis, golf, horseback riding, and fishing.

Georgesland
Rem and Joan Joy
Dualla/Kilkenny Road
Cashel, County Tipperary
Telephone and **FAX:** 062-62788
Bedrooms: 6; 3 with private baths, 3 with shared.
Rates: £18.50 private; £16.50 shared; Single: £20-22; discount for children. Vouchers accepted. Dinner is available for £13. **Credit cards:** None. **Open:** March 1 to October 31. **Children:** Yes. **Pets:** No. **Smoking:** No. **Provision for handicapped:** None. **Directions:** From Cashel Tourist Office go to Friar Street. Pass R.C. Church on left. Take next left (R691) opposite Citroen garage. Travel 1 mile Georgesland is on right.

This modern country bungalow is set in a peaceful landscaped garden just a kilometer from the famous Rock of Cashel and Bru Boru Heritage Centre. As you drive in you will be greeted by a bevy of beautiful blooming roses. The lovely, nicely decorated, and comfortable rooms are outfitted with orthopedic beds. The lounge has a TV. The breakfast is your choice of full Irish or continental. There is a secure car park. Nearby you will find fishing, golf, horseback riding, forest walks and tours.

Inch House
John and Nora Egan
Thurles, County Tipperary
Telephone: 0504-51348/51261; **FAX:** 0504-51348
Bedrooms: 5, all with private baths.
Rates: £25 p.p.; Single £1 extra; 20 percent discount for children.
Vouchers not accepted. £22.50 dinner. **Credit cards:** VISA, Access,
MasterCard, Eurocard. **Open:** All year except Christmas week. **Children:** Yes. **Pets:** No. **Smoking:** Yes. **Provision for handicapped:** None.
Directions: From Thurles, take top righthand side of square to
Neuagh Road. Drive 4½ miles, and Inch House is signposted on the
left.

This elegant, 1717 restored Georgian manor house was in the Ryan
family for 300 years until it was bought by the Egans. The high ceiling, large windows, and lovely antiques will capture your admiration.
Stained-glass windows look onto a curving stairway to bedrooms that
are roomy and have high-back antique beds. The dining room has
classic red and green decor, and there is a restaurant open to the public for dinners with prime meats, game, and fresh fish served. The sitting room has a Persian rug, a fireplace, and magnificent plaster
ceiling designs. Relax here and read or chat. Full Irish Breakfast with
homemade breads and fresh fruit salad with rhubarb and stawberries
is offered. It is only minutes to the Rock of Cashel, Glen of Aherlow,
Galtee Mountains, and Lough Derg for fishing and water sports.

ALSO RECOMMENDED

Bansha, *Bansha Castle Country House,* John and Theresa Russell, off N24 on the right coming south into Bansha Village. Telephone and FAX: 062-54187. Bedrooms: 6, 4 with private baths. Large handsome mansion restored to original beauty set on large grassy fields with sheep and horses grazing. Convenient for touring beautiful Glen of Aherlow. Fishing and horseback riding available nearby.

Cashel, *Ros-Guill House,* Mrs. Evelyn Mooney, Dualla Road. Telephone: 052-01507. Bedrooms: 5, 3 with private baths. Vouchers accepted. Credit cards accepted. Open April through October. Elegant country home overlooking Rock of Cashel. Won the Galtee Award in 1987. Recommended by Eileen Kelly of Clontarf, County Dublin.

Cashel, *Thornbrook House,* Mrs. Mary Kennedy, Dualla Road. Telephone: 062-62388. Bedrooms: 5, 3 en suite. Vouchers accepted. Lovely ranch-type family home on country road 1 km out of Cashel. Modern and well run B&B. Recommended by many of our other B&B owners. Just northeast of Cashel on the R691 in country setting. Ask for directions from town to find this road. Not clearly signposted.

County Waterford

Waterford is a small county in the South most noted for its superb Waterford Crystal Factory in the town of Waterford on the eastern rim. The Visitors' Center's lavish displays and the handling of the public are a bit Disneyesque. We were disappointed that we couldn't take photos of the glassblowers as that was quite fascinating, as well as the delicate and careful etching work. We only saw men working there and wondered where the women artisans were. It is a pleasant enough city to see with plenty of medieval towers and old walls. Visit the Reginald Tower Museum, the Waterford Heritage Center, and the New Ross Gallery. The Tourist Office is on the quay on the Suir River bordering the northern edge of town. We had a fine and reasonable Irish lunch at The Olde Stand Restaurant at 45 Michael St. It's a big Victorian place with etched glass doors and inside are cozy benches and tables and a long, lit-up center buffet and carvery with servers. The choices of light or heavy meals were quite varied.

Curraghmore House is a good visit just outside Portlaw. To the east are the rough and pretty Cheekpoint and Passage East with its car ferry to Arthurstown in Wexford, and its water views, wild goats, and numerous water birds to study. Dunmore East, farther south, has picturesque coves and swimming and snorkeling. Tramore, a tourist town on the ocean, has a 3-mile beach and huge amusement park. North from Waterford Town it's a straight shot to Kilkenny and northeast it's only 45 miles to Cashel in Tipperary, with its exciting castle rising out of the rock.

To the west, towards Cork, is one of the most charming towns in Ireland, and that is Ardmore. Here, you'll find a glorious sweep of a beach and on the hill is a very high Norman round tower and Celtic-cross cemetery with fantastic views of the beach and the countryside beyond. It's a nice spot to just sit and meditate. There is a bakery on the west side of the main street that is open in summer, where you'll find "melt in your mouth" hot scones and an adorable garden with tables in the back. Back out on the N25, there are some wonderful dairy farms with views of the ocean. Some are bed and breakfasts listed in this book.

Newtown View Farm
Teresa O'Connor
Grange
Ardmore, County Waterford
Telephone and **FAX:** 024-94143
Bedrooms: 6, all with private baths.
Rates: £17 p.p.; Single £22; 50 percent discount for children under 12.
Vouchers accepted. £12 dinner. **Credit cards:** VISA, MasterCard, Euro-
card. **Open:** March 1 to November 1. **Children:** All ages. **Pets:** In shed.
Smoking: No. **Provision for handicapped:** Yes. **Directions:** From Ard-
more, take the N25 east and turn south at Fleming's Pub. The farm-
house is ¼ mile on left.

This stunning modern house on a dairy farm in lovely country surroundings has views on all sides. Teresa is very friendly and energetic.
She uses a lot of pink flowers in her room colors, as well as blue and
green floral designs. In the back there are farm animals, ducks, and
guinea hens for children to visit. The O'Connors also have their own
tennis court on the property. The lounge is cozy with a peat fire and
the dining room has a pink theme. In her Irish Breakfast, Teresa offers
a choice of eggs, beans on toast, and a buffet with juice, fresh fruit,
and cereals. There are swimming, golf, tennis, and ponytrekking in
the area. A children's pony is available. The farm is also close to the
sea, handy for fishing. You may easily visit the towns of Ardmore, with
its Norman Tower, and medieval Youghal.

Summerhill Farmhouse
Sheila Budd
Kinsalebeg
Ardmore, County Waterford
Telephone: 024-92682
Bedrooms: 6; 4 with private baths, 2 with shared.
Rates: £17.50 p.p.; Single £21-22.50; 25 percent discount for children under 12. Vouchers accepted. £12 dinner. **Credit cards:** VISA, MasterCard. **Open:** March 1 to October 31. **Children:** Yes, all ages. **Pets:** No. **Smoking:** Restricted to lounge. **Provision for handicapped:** Yes.
Directions: On the N25 going east, watch for the Summerhill sign on the left, about 2-3 km after the bridge crossing the Blackwater River outside Youghal. Or coming west on the N25, it is 1.5 km after Grange on the right.

The Budd family will greet you with the most warm welcome you can get in this part of Ireland. This modern farmhouse, with a new lounge with cathedral ceiling and big bay-window view of the Atlantic Ocean beyond the green pasture, is extraordinary. The superb breakfasts are served in the modern dining room with separate tables, and the dinners are equally scrumptious. We enjoyed watching the cows coming up the meadow and the cats being fed the fresh milk. It's a happy family where Sheila manages the bed and breakfast inside and her husband tends the livestock outside. However, it wasn't always that way; as newlyweds they worked side by side doing the chores. You'll love the comfortable bedrooms and the side trips: the beach at Ardmore, the medieval walled city of Youghal, the Blackwater for fishing. Or just relax with a good book in the very beautiful conservatory with a fireplace and pretty blue velvet chairs. Other special bonuses are the pony cart rides around the farm and the miniature golf course by the barn.

Glencree
Rena Power
The Sweep
Kilmeaden, County Waterford
Telephone: 051-384240
Bedrooms: 5; 4 with private baths, 1 with shared.
Rates: £17 p.p. private bath; £15 p.p. shared bath; Single £22; 20 percent discount for children under 12. Vouchers accepted. **Credit cards:** None. **Open:** March 1 to November 30. **Children:** All ages. **Pets:** In shed. **Smoking:** Restricted. **Provision for handicapped:** None. **Directions:** From Dungarvan, traveling east on the N25, pass the Waterford Coop, go 500 yards farther to the Texaco station, take a sharp right, go a few hundred yards, and take a right at the signpost for Glencree; the stone-wall entrance is on the right.

Glencree means "heart of the glen" and it is a lovely modern home with a very kind and happy family running it. If you arrive late, Mr. Power will join you for tea and a happy chat until Rena returns from her walk and joins you. You can't help noticing the crystal chandeliers in the hall and the lounge, which is very roomy. They get CNN News on their TV. The rooms are comfy with flowered duvets in pink, rose, blue, white and orange, and green and champagne. One room has a sheepskin rug. A section of the lounge serves as the dining room where Rena will serve you an Irish Breakfast varied with choice of eggs, French toast, cheese, yogurt, and cereal. There is one big table and a small one. They are only 8 minutes from the Waterford Crystal Factory. Beaches are only 15 minutes away and so is horseback riding, golf, and greyhound racing. (One English guest staying at Glencree told us he raised racing greyhounds and had them housed in kennels in Waterford. He loved his dogs and visited them as often as he could.)

Cloneen
Neil and Maria Skedd
Love Lane
Tramore, County Waterford
Telephone: 051-381264
Bedrooms: 3, all with private baths.
Rates: £16-£17 p.p.; Single £20; 50 percent discount for children.
Vouchers accepted. £12 dinner. **Credit cards:** VISA and MasterCard.
Open: March to November. **Children:** All ages. **Pets:** No. **Smoking:** No.
Provision for handicapped: Yes. **Directions:** Stay on the main Waterford-Tramore road. Go up a steep hill, keeping the coast on your left.
Take the next left to Love Lane.

This pretty white bungalow, on one acre, is surrounded by rose trellises and gardens and has secure parking. Tramore is a lovely country section of Waterford not far from the ocean. Maria gives you the traditional Irish Breakfast with a choice of cereals, scrambled or poached eggs, fresh fruit, and yogurt. This home is close to golf courses, tennis courts, and scenic walks to the beautiful, golden beaches with many seaside attractions, including a 50-acre amusement park. You can rent a bike in town and discover miles of quiet country roads. The famous Waterford Crystal Factory and store is a short drive away.

Glenorney
Marie Murphy
Newtown
Tramore, County Waterford
Telephone: 052-381056; **FAX:** 051-381103
Bedrooms: 6, all with private baths.
Rates: £17.50-20 p.p., Single £23-25; 20 percent discount for children.
Vouchers accepted. **Credit cards:** Yes. **Open:** March 1 to November 30.
Children: Yes, 5 and upwards. **Pets:** No. **Smoking:** No. **Provision for
handicapped:** Yes. **Directions:** From Tramore town, go south on the
coast road (R675). Glenorney is opposite the Tramore Golf Club.

This is a spacious and luxurious home with spectacular views of
Tramore Bay. Pretty bedrooms are done in pastel shades with peaches,
pinks, and greens and one room in blue and yellow. The lounge and
dining room is done in pink and green. An extraordinary home-
cooked breakfast menu is served. You have a choice of fruit, cereal,
and the Irish cooked breakfast, but you also have a choice of hot kippers with tomatoes, special French toast, baked beans, or pancakes
with maple syrup. After this sumptuous breakfast you can tackle
nearby Splashworld to use up some of the extra energy. The Murphys
will suggest other recreational options as they pride themselves on
attending to every detail so your stay is enjoyable and relaxing. Marie
would like you to think of the Glenorney as your home away from
home.

Seaview Lodge
Frances and Cyril Darcy
Seaview Park
Tramore, County Waterford
Telephone and **FAX:** 051-381122
Bedrooms: 5, all with private baths.
Rates: £17 p.p.; Single £23; 25 percent discount for children under 12.
Vouchers accepted. **Credit cards:** Yes. **Open:** March 15 to October
31. **Children:** Yes, over 4 years. **Pets:** No. **Smoking:** In lounge only. **Provision for handicapped:** Yes. **Directions:** Follow the R675 south from
Waterford to Tramore. Travel 6 miles to the Maxol Station. Take the
first right at the signpost to Seaview Lodge. Coming from Cork, take
the N25. After Kilmeaden Village, take the R682 to the right to
Tramore. At the next small roundabout you will see Seaview Lodge.

This spacious bungalow with a spectacular view of the Atlantic
ocean and extensive gardens has two family bedrooms and three doubles or twins. The rooms are fully equipped with TVs, tea and coffee
makers, and hairdryers. The Darcys offer a special menu that includes
pancakes, omelettes, and smoked kippers or the full Irish Breakfast.
Nearby is golf, fishing, and nighttime entertainment. You are only 7
minutes from the Waterford Crystal Factory. Mrs. Darcy is an exceptional hostess in every regard. Investigate the sandy beach of Tramore,
or motor to Dungarvan and see some beautiful seascapes. Mrs. Darcy
will advise you on how to proceed and what to see.

Annvill House
Phyllis O'Reilly
The Orchard, Kingsmeadow
Waterford Town, County Waterford
Telephone: 051-373617
Bedrooms: 5; 4 with private baths, 1 with private not in room.
Rates: £16.50 p.p.; Single £27; 10 percent discount for children under 12. Vouchers accepted. **Credit cards:** None. **Open:** January 3 to December 22. **Children:** Age 7 and older. **Pets:** No. **Smoking:** No. **Provision for handicapped:** None. **Directions:** From Cork, take a left just after the Crystal Factory, go to the roundabout, make a left turn, go 1 block and left again; the house is the first on the left, at the corner of Ashe Street.

This attractive, modern 2-story home is very near the Crystal Factory. Phyllis will bring you tea or coffee on arrival in her pleasant lounge with a TV. If you wish, she has a video/film available of the factory, plus a 3-hour touring film of Ireland. Her rooms are good sized with some brass beds and flowered quilts in purple, yellow, or brown. In her dining room you'll see a glass display case, lit up, with treasures of Waterford crystal collected and received as gifts over the years. Besides the standard Irish Breakfast, she likes to serve potato waffles, the frozen kind. In the area, there is indoor bowling, a walking tour of the city, and Irish caeli dancing. Visit the singing pub, *Mullan's.* Also golf, swimming beaches, and indoor bowling are nearby.

ALSO RECOMMENDED

Dungarvan, *Seaview,* Mrs. Nora Fahey, Windgap Pulla, Youghal Road, Dungarvan West. Telephone: 058-41583. Bedrooms: 5, 3 with private baths. Lovely bungalow perched on the hill alongside N25 as the highway descends into city, with sweeping view of Dungarvan Bay.

Nire Valley, *Hanora's Country Cottage,* Seamus and Mary Wall, Nire Valley via Clonmel. Telephone: 051-81497. Bedrooms: 5, all with private baths. Evening meals à la carte. Beautifully redecorated ancestral home in peaceful setting. Superb meals. Golf nearby. Near Ballymacarbry, south of Clonmel. Very scenic region to tour!

County Westmeath

County Westmeath in the Lakelands area is a perfect place to stay to see the Midlands of Ireland. It is a small county with Lough Ennel and Lough Owel near Mullingar in the center, and it has the great Lough Ree along its western edge, which is part of the River Shannon waterway going to the north and south. This is a good county for country walks and bicycling. There is fishing and boating in the lakes and golf in Mullingar, Athlone, Moate, and Birr. You'll find County Westmeath is made up mostly of farmlands, and Mullingar is called the "cattle capital" of Ireland. Much cattle trading is done here, also. In Mullingar, visit the beautiful carved-stone Christ the King Cathedral, and just 5 km south of town be sure to see the Belvedere House Gardens, with its enticing view of the islands of Lough Ennel from its terraced and walled gardens. You'll enjoy the 1790s pub in town called Canten Casey's. On the road from Mullingar to Kells there is a dairy and pig farm that children will adore called the Ben Breeze Open Farm. There are splendid birds to see there also.

North of Mullingar, at Castlepollard, are the Tullynally Castle and Gardens, where the earls of Langford lived, and the Fore Abbey and St. Fechin's 10th-century church in the town of Fore. To the southeast, Athlone is a popular town, being on the N6, the much-traveled road between Galway and Dublin. It stands between Lough Ree and the River Shannon and the views are lovely. Here is where the famous Irish tenor John McCormack was born; and here is where the Irish retreated after the Battle of the Boyne. Visit the handsome Norman 13th-century Athlone Castle and the and the Athlone Crystal showroom. Due east of Athlone is the town of Moate with its golf and horseback riding. Farther east you may explore the interesting and historical Kilbeggan Distillery and Museum. Other houses with lovely gardens to visit are Emo Court, Birr Castle, Clonalis House at Castlerea, and Abbeyleix at Woodland Gardens.

Hounslow House
Eithne Healy
Fore
Castlepollard, County Westmeath
Telephone: 044-61144; **FAX:** 044-61847
Bedrooms: 6; 5 with private bath, 1 with shared.
Rates: £16 p.p. private bath; £14 shared bath; Single £5 extra; 50 percent discount for children. £1 dinner. Vouchers accepted. **Credit cards:** None. **Open:** March 1 to November 30. **Children:** Yes, all ages. **Pets:** No. **Smoking:** No. **Provision for handicapped:** None. **Directions:** On the L49, 4 miles north of Castlepollard, and 6 miles south of Oldcastle. Follow signs from Village of Fore, 1.5 km out.

We don't have many farms in our book, but we have selected a few where you can see a working farm in action and get a taste of Irish farming. We enjoy them a lot and hope you will too. This lovely 200-year-old farmhouse is located on wooded heights overlooking the beautiful valley of Fore, and its historic abbey. Two bedrooms have wooden floors decorated with pretty curtains and matching duvet covers and pillow cases. Three bedrooms have wall to wall carpets and are equally color coordinated. Tea or coffee is offered for a real farm welcome on your arrival. There are many amenities: babysitting, hairdryers in the rooms, tea- and coffee-making facilities in bedrooms, computers, table tennis and pool tables in the game room. You can visit Tullynally Castle and Lough Lene, and Loughcrew cairns nearby. An eighteen-hole golf course also nearby.

Hilltop Country House
Sean and Dympna Casey
Delvin Road (N52), Rathconnell
Mullingar, County Westmeath
Telephone: 044-48958; **FAX:** 044-48013
Bedrooms: 5, all with private baths.
Rates: £18 p.p.; Single £6.50 extra. Vouchers accepted. **Credit cards:** None. **Open:** All year, except Christmas. **Children:** Negotiable. **Pets:** No. **Smoking:** Restricted. **Provision for handicapped:** One room is suitable. **Directions:** From Dublin, take second exit off N4 to Mullingar (not town center) N52/Delvin Road.

This lovely, modern, split-level bungalow, situated in the Lakeland District, is a haven of peace and tranquility. The house has a long porch across the front and terraced gardens. All rooms, comfortably decorated in a mix of antiques and modern furniture, have TVs and original watercolors. The colors are pink and cocoa, rose and white, or pastel flowered. Some have country views or garden views. The splendid gardens, front and back, have a wide variety of trees, shrubs, and flowers. The traditional Irish Breakfast Dympna serves includes a choice of cereals, fresh fruits and compotes, fresh orange juice, and special requests. There is a tea and coffee buffet in the corridor. This house is ideally located as a base for visiting many historical sights such as Christ the King Cathedral and the Military and Historical Museum, or Columb Barracks. There is golf, fishing, and horseback riding available locally. The interior of Canton Casey's Pub, in town, has been kept the same as when it began in the 1790s.

ALSO RECOMMENDED

Athlone, *Harbour House,* Mrs. Bernadette Keegan, Ballykeeran (1.5 km off N55). Telephone: 0902-85063. Bedrooms: 6, all with private baths. Vouchers accepted. All major credit cards. Golf, fishing, sailing on Lough Ree, horseback riding.

Moate, *Temple,* Declan and Bernadette Fagan, Horseleap (4 miles east of Moate on N6). Telephone and FAX: 0506-35118. Bedrooms: 4, all with private baths. VISA, MasterCard. Beautiful Victorian farmhouse with lovely garden in parkland setting.

COUNTY WEXFORD

County Wexford

Wexford is the southeasternmost county and has a strong tie to England with its ferries crossing from Rosslare Harbor. Ferries also cross from here to LeHavre and Cherbourg, France. Wexford City was a major Viking trading center and is full of medieval buildings. It is quite sophisticated and very proud of its arts and culture centers. They have an Opera Festival for a week every October and enjoy presenting unfamiliar operas. During that week, they have art shows and musical features all over town, a whole program to suit all kinds of people. You should visit Johnstown Castle just south of the city. At Raven Point, across the harbor, is the Wexford Wildlife Reserve.

To the north is Enniscorthy, which has a Strawberry Fair Festival each year at the end of June. You may fish the Slaney River and visit the castle, museum, and famous potters of the area. From Wexford, right on the Irish Sea, drive west to historical New Ross over rolling green hills and farmlands. New Ross is on the River Barrow and has great fishing. The John F. Kennedy Arboretum is a lovely place to visit in this town.

The southwest area has many waterways and at Arthurstown you may take a quaint car ferry across to Passage East in Waterford. Ride down to view the beautiful lighthouse at Hook Head. Two features you can enjoy as a tourist throughout County Wexford are great golf courses and horseback riding.

Ballinkeele House
John and Margaret Maher
Ballymurn
Enniscorthy, County Wexford
Telephone: 053-38105; **FAX:** 053-38468; **E-mail:** Balnkeeleindigo.ie
Bedrooms: 5, all with private baths.
Rates: £35-45 p.p.; Single £10 extra; discount for children. Vouchers not accepted. £20 dinner. **Credit cards:** VISA, MasterCard/Access, Barclay. **Open:** March 1 to November 12. **Children:** All ages. **Pets:** No. **Smoking:** Restricted. **Provision for handicapped:** None. **Directions:** N11 north to Oilgate village and turn right at the signpost. From Enniscorthy, take N11 south to Oilgate village, turn left at the signpost. Follow the signs to Ballymurn, turn left at the sign; it's the 2nd gate on the left.

This ancestral home of the Maher family is gray Wicklow granite, built in 1840 in the Georgian style. It is set amidst 360 acres of woodlands and farmlands and is grand with high ceilings and very large rooms. Soft Oriental rugs grace the front entrance hall and family portraits and original antique furniture are in all rooms. Some beds are 4 poster with canopies, and all have farmland views. It has not changed over the years and still has the air of a country mansion. Besides the full Irish Breakfast, you'll get yogurt, pancakes, homemade soda bread, and jams. A formal gourmet dinner is served in the beautiful dining room with a set menu. The entrées are 4-star, haute cuisine, and must be booked early on day of arrival. The dinner is followed by coffee and tea in the drawing room on a handmade table. There is croquet, a billiard table, and an all-weather tennis court at Ballinkeele and there are good walks on the grounds and fishing nearby. The town is 10 km away. It is not far from the coast or the tourist attractions of Wexford City.

Woodlands Farmhouse
Philomena O'Sullivan
Killinierin
Gorey, County Wexford
Telephone: 0402-37125; **FAX:** 0402-37133
Bedrooms: 6, all with private baths.
Rates: £20 p.p.; 50 percent discount for children. Vouchers accepted.
£12-16 dinner; £9 high tea. **Credit cards:** Yes. **Open:** April 1 to November 1. **Children:** Yes. **Pets:** No. **Smoking:** No. **Provision for handicapped:** None. **Directions:** From Gorey, take N11 north for 3 miles to the signpost for Woodlands on the left. Take the road in to Killinierin for 3 km. The house is on the left with a sign (1 km from Killinierin).

This is a beautiful, white, stucco farmhouse with a fascinating bit of history that Philomena will eventually tell you if you have the time for a good story. The hostess has a wonderful sense of humor and is very helpful too. The house is tucked away from hustle and bustle. The rooms are decorated in peach and pink with fine taste, and all have garden or panoramic countryside views; three of the rooms have balconies. The sitting room is handsomely situated with many antiques, and the dining room has green flowered drapes and pink tablecloths, as well as large windows with views of prize gardens. Philomena serves a full Irish Breakfast with choices from the menu. Tea and scones are always served upon your arrival. There is a pool table, and there are tennis courts on the property, along with a few cattle and a horse. Pony rides are offered to the children. Killinierin is an interesting town to visit, and there is a local pub 10 minutes away. There are also singing lounges and dancing in the area. The owners will babysit. Try their 3- or 5-course farm fresh, home-cooked dinners. Your stay should be wonderful.

Cypress House Farm
Nancy and James Wall
Newbawn, County Wexford
Telephone: 051-428335
Bedrooms: 5, all with private baths.
Rates: £15 p.p.; 50 percent discount for children under 12. Vouchers accepted. **Credit cards:** None. **Open:** February 1 to November 30. **Children:** All ages. **Pets:** In shed. **Smoking:** Restricted. **Provision for handicapped:** None. **Directions:** From Wexford, take the N25 for 12 miles, follow the signs to Newbawn, and look for a *brown* signpost on the left. Stay to the left toward Newbawn for 2 miles and follow the brown signs for Cypress House Farm.

This 1920s 2-story farmhouse has a pretty wooden door at its entry. The large windows give you beautiful views of country farmlands. On these 130 acres, the Walls grow grain and hay. James and Nancy are very friendly and James showed us around the big yard where they have a new tennis court with a walking path around it and a croquet field. The oversized living room has original paintings and we enjoyed tea and delicious scones by a fire in the fireplace. The rooms have good views and are bright and very nicely decorated in ivory, pinks, and greens. Some have Embroidery Anglais; one has a satin coverlet. A new bedroom has a balcony, and there is a new conservatory in the back and garden walks. The dining room has antique furniture and here you will be served the full Irish Breakfast, which we hope includes those scones. Besides the tennis court, there is horseback riding on the property and ponies for children. There are forest walks, golf, fishing, and boating on the River Barrow within 6 or 7 miles. The town of New Ross has many tourist attractions.

Ardruadh
Jim and Colette Cahill
Spawell Road
Wexford, County Wexford
Telephone and **FAX:** 053-23194
Bedrooms: 6, all with private baths.
Rates: £18-22 p.p.; Single £20-28; discount for children. Vouchers not accepted. **Credit cards:** VISA, MasterCard/Access. **Open:** All year, except 1 week at Christmas. **Children:** Ages 3 and up. **Pets.** No. **Smoking:** Restricted. **Provision for handicapped:** None. **Directions:** From Wexford City, follow the N25 to Spawell Road and go right. The house is directly on your left; go into the yard and park in the back.

This fascinating building was built by an Irish timber merchant in 1893, who saw a house he liked in Norway and had the plans, stones, and wood sent back to Ireland. It has many gables and a handsome wooden arch design over the front doorway. Original doors and windows are paraná pine. Of the rooms, one has 2 big bay windows looking out to the Slaney River with colors of pink and hot fuchsia in lacey trims. Colors used in other rooms are peach, pastel blues, and green. The Corishes, very cordial, ran a hotel in New Ross once and lived in America for 12 years. The oversized sitting room has a French ornate couch, a baby grand piano, and other lovely antiques. The red and white dining room has a view of the river. Offerings are full Irish, choices of eggs, tomatoes, mushrooms, muesli, and grapefruit. You'll find tennis, golf, boating, fishing, horse racing and riding, opera, theater, and movies nearby. Also, see the Bird Sanctuary, Johnstown Castle, Heritage Park, and art museums. Rosslare Ferry is 12 miles away.

Clonard House
Kathleen Hayes
Clonard Great
Wexford, County Wexford
Telephone: 053-43141 or 053-41337; **FAX:** 053-43141
Bedrooms: 9, all with private baths. There is one extra bathroom with bathtub.
Rates: £20 p.p.; Single £25; 50 percent discount for children. Vouchers accepted. £14 dinner. **Credit cards:** Yes. **Children:** All ages. **Pets:** No. **Provision for handicapped:** No. **Directions:** On the Wexford Ring Road, go to the R733/N25 roundabout. Take R733 south and first road on left, which is Farm Road. The Clonard House is signposted.

This luxurious Georgian farmhouse, part of a dairy farm, has a very friendly host and hostess. Their daughter, Avril, served us delicious Irish coffee on arrival, and they were very generous with suggestions of where to eat in Wexford. This is a working dairy farm of 60 cows, and it is enjoyable to see them line up morning and night to be milked in the barn. Some rooms have a far away view of Wexford Bay, and others face various parts of the farm estate. A full Irish Breakfast is served with a choice of smoked salmon and scrambled eggs or buffet. There is a castle view on the property where Cromwell lived. See the Heritage Park nearby or visit the old cultural seaport of Wexford. There are many good restaurants in town.

O'Brien's Auburn House
David and Mary O'Brien
2 Auburn Terrace
Redmond Road
Wexford Town, County Wexford
Telephone: 053-23605
Bedrooms: 5; 4 with private baths, 1 with shared.
Rates: £17-18 p.p.; Single £21-23; 50 percent discount for children under 12. Vouchers not accepted. **Credit cards:** VISA, MasterCard.
Open: All year, except December 22 to January 1. **Children:** All ages.
Pets: No. **Smoking:** Restricted. **Provision for handicapped:** None.
Directions: Take the N25 to Dunnes Stores in Wexford. After Dunnes and in front of the railway station, take the first left to Redmond Road, a street parallel to the river. About 50 yards down and across from the cinema, it is the second red brick house on left.

This charming Victorian 1891 house was elegantly restored in 1991 to the highest standards by the O'Briens. Mary and David take pride in looking after their guests. We liked the high ceilings, large rooms, and Edwardian decor. All of the bedrooms now have TVs and tea- and coffee-making facilities. The Opera Festival was on when we were there, and a couple from England described how they had researched all the B&Bs in Wexford and picked this one. Soft pastels are used in long drapes, quilts, and rugs to give bedrooms a stately touch. Large baths with showers remind us of continental pensions. The young couple are a delight and anxious to please. Their breakfast is served in a large dining room through glass doors off the fireplaced lounge. The breakfast is the full Irish one but cereals, yogurts, cheeses, and a choice of eggs. Amenities within short distances are the beaches, golf, horseback riding, swimming, Heritage Park, and Johnstown Castle. The house has a private car park.

ALSO RECOMMENDED

Enniscorthy, *Oakville Lodge,* Mrs. Attracta Doyle, Mountfinn Lane, Ballycarney. Telephone: 054-88626. Bedrooms: 5, 3 with private baths. Vouchers accepted. VISA accepted. Country location overlooking Slaney River Valley. Individual porches outside of three rooms to view pretty landscaped garden. It also has an attractive conservatory.

New Ross, *Rosville House,* Philomena Gallagher, off N25 1 km from New Ross on the Wexford Road. Telephone 051-421798. Bedrooms 5, 4 with private baths. Modern bungalow in Knockmullen set on the hillside overlooking Barrow River Valley. Nice border of roses in front. Car park in rear. Sunny breakfast room when we were there. Pleasant hostess.

County Wicklow

County Wicklow is unique and notable especially for its starring feature of the wooded Glendalough Mountains and Valley, and the 7th- to 14th-century ruins of St. Kevin's Monastery. With its chapel, cathedral, round tower, and fine old Celtic crosses laid out over acres of greenery, it is awe inspiring. Its new Visitor Center informs you of the whole history with films, models, and pictures.

The other special feature of this county is its location so central to Dublin, Kilkenny, and the coast, and it contains the direct route to County Wexford in the south. Wicklow Town, right on the Irish Sea, has ruins and castles of its own in addition to good beaches. South of Wicklow and Glendalough, at Avondale Forest Park, is a peaceful place called "Meeting of the Waters," named for a poem of Thomas Moore, where you may hear traditional Irish music every day in season. Here you may visit Avondale House, the home of the great Irish patriot, Charles Parnell. Visit the extensive Powerscourt Gardens, the pride of Wicklow.

In the same area is the town of Avoca, home of Avoca Handwoven Woolen Goods. At the Craft Shop, you may watch a weaver working at his or her loom. Working farther south you'll enjoy the boats and quays of the fishing town of Arklow. Visit the Arklow Pottery Factory and Craft Shop. Take a walk on Brittas Bay Beach and visit the Maritime Museum.

In the northwest corner of the county is the tiny town of Russborough on a lake, which proudly displays the Russborough House, an elaborate baroque, granite house, built in the 1740s that has paintings by famous European artists. Ashford, to the north of Wicklow Town, is known for its lovely Mount Usher Gardens abloom with azaleas and rhododendrons in the spring. Traveling northeast, you'll want to take the marvelous refreshing hilltop walk along Bray Head with its panoramic ocean views.

Greenfields
Conor Moloney
Blainroe, County Wicklow
Telephone: 0404-68309
Bedrooms: 5, all with private baths.
Rates: £17 p.p.; Single £20; 25 percent discount for children. Vouchers not accepted. **Credit cards:** None. **Open:** January 1 to December 31. **Children:** Yes, all ages. **Pets:** No. **Smoking:** Yes. **Provision for handicapped:** None. **Directions:** Go 5 miles out on coast road (Dunbar Road), south of Wicklow Town. Greenfields is the first house on the left after Blainroe Golf Club.

This beautiful ranch-style bungalow stands on one and a half acres, with a spring pond in the garden, in a gorgeous setting with views of the ocean. There is a nice sunny guest lounge where tea or coffee is served. The rooms are beautifully decorated in blues and greens, pinks, or blue and white. Guests may also use the sun room facing the Irish sea, or the game room with pool table. There is an extensive breakfast menu served in their handsome dining room; breakfast includes the full Irish Breakfast plus cheeses, yogurts, both puddings, peppered mackerel, and smoked kippers. Go to the beach or sun in the garden, play golf at the championship course next door, go horseback riding 10 km away, take walks downtown, and by all means go hear the traditional Irish music played daily at the "Meeting of the Waters" near Avondale, 8 miles south of town. Avondale is the home of the famous Irish patriot, Charles Parnell. Donald Hunt, author of *To the Greenfields Beyond,* has stayed here.

Carmel's
Carmel Hawkins
Annamoe
Glendalough, County Wicklow
Telephone and **FAX:** 0404-45297
Bedrooms: 4; 3 with private baths, 1 with shared.
Rates: £17 p.p. private bath; Single £27; 25 percent discount for children. Vouchers not accepted. **Credit cards:** None. **Open:** March 1 to October 31. **Children:** All ages. **Pets:** No. **Smoking:** No. **Provision for handicapped:** Yes. **Directions:** From Dublin, take the N11 to the signpost for Glendalough, go to Laragh Village, and follow the fingerpost sign to Carmel's or ask at any shop in Annamoe.

This home is family run and has been extended to make rooms for the B&B. The Hawkinses are known for their hospitality and congeniality. Set in the heart of the breathtaking Wicklow Mountains, it will give you a break from the hustle and bustle of cities. All the rooms are pretty, clean, neat, and tastefully decorated. Fresh flowers adorn them and for that homey feeling, Carmel has electric blankets and hairdryers for each room. The lounge has a TV and it has been extended. In the dining room you will be given a real Irish Breakfast along with different ideas like fresh fruit salad, home-baked muffins, and cheeses of different countries. The B&B is only 1 hour to the ferry to England, 1½ hours to Dublin City or Dublin Airport, and 17 miles to Bray Head. It is 10 miles to Wicklow Town, and only 7 miles to the well-known mountains and woods of the splendid Glendalough, with its monastic ruins in the valley, ancient chapel, round tower, and numbers of Celtic crosses. Some of the ruins date back to the 7th century when St. Kevin founded the monastery. You will not want to miss this awesome sight with its informative Visitor Center.

Rosita
Rita Byrne
Dunbur Park
Wicklow Town, County Wicklow
Telephone: 0404-67059
Bedrooms: 4, all with private baths.
Rates: £16; Single £22; 20 percent discount for children. Vouchers accepted. **Credit cards:** None. **Open:** All year except Christmas. **Children:** Yes. **Pets:** No. **Smoking:** No. **Provision for handicapped:** None.
Directions: Drive through town center toward Summerhill, on to Dunbur Road. At the pedestrian crossing, turn right into Dunbur Park; it's the last bungalow on the right.

A warm welcome greets you at this friendly modern Georgian bungalow overlooking Wicklow Bay, where Rita and her husband George have been hosting B&B guests for over twenty years. This is a popular place with many Irish travelers, returning each year. It is surrounded by a lovely garden where the garden motif continues into the home with pink and green, pale blue and lemon, pink and white, and pink and gray lovely, flowered bedrooms. The lounge has a large TV where tea, coffee, and hot scones with homemade jam are served. The dining room has separate tables with nice mahogany furniture looking out onto patio and garden. A full Irish Breakfast is served with additional items such as cheeses, yogurts, fresh fruit, porridge, and cereals. Here you will be treated as family.

Silver Sands
Lyla Doyle
Dunbur Road
Wicklow, County Wicklow
Telephone: 0404-68243
Bedrooms: 5; 3 with private baths, 2 with shared.
Rates: £18.50 p.p. private bath; £16 p.p. shared bath; Single £21-23; 50 percent discount for children under 12. Vouchers accepted. **Credit cards:** None. **Open:** All year, except 4 days at Christmas. **Children:** All ages. **Pets:** No. **Smoking:** Restricted. **Provision for handicapped:** None. **Directions:** From Wicklow town center, take the coast road (Dunbar Road) 3½ km and the house is on the right.

Silver Sands is a bungalow with a front garden that overlooks the Irish Sea and Sugarloaf Mountains. You can see all the way from Bray Head in the north to Wicklow Head Golf Course in the south. Lyla's rooms are very attractive with pink roses, pink and wine designs, green, and an unusual black and rose coverlet in one room. Rooms en suite have TVs and coffee-making facilities. All rooms have tea-making facilities. The dining room in front has spectacular ocean views and the lounge is quite comfortable. Breakfast extras are choice of eggs, fruits, yogurts, and herring. There are cliff walks and a walk to the harbor across the street from the house that goes by the Black Castle ruins. Beaches and fishing are very nearby. Golf is across the street and horseback riding is 4 minutes away in Ashford. Lyla suggested (and we tried) the Grand Hotel for dinner and it was reasonable and very good.

ALSO RECOMMENDED

Bray, *Rosslyn House,* Peggy Kelly. On Killarney Road just south up the street from Bray Town Hall. Telephone: 01-2860993; FAX: 01-2862419. 3 Bedrooms, 2 with private baths. Elegant Victorian in quiet location, within walking distance of restaurants, pubs, and shops. Private car park. Convenient to DART.

Coolgreaney, *Ballykilty Farmhouse,* Mrs. A. Nuzum. From Arklow take Coolgreaney Road at the roundabout and follow the same road for three miles. Ballykilty is the yellow farmhouse on the right. Telephone: 0402-37111. Beautiful, peaceful garden surrounds house. Old-fashioned fireplace in dining room. Won Farmhouse of the Year award. Working dairy farm with other farm animals in rear pasture. Mrs. Nuzum is a pleasant and accommodating hostess.

Northern Ireland

NORTHERN IRELAND

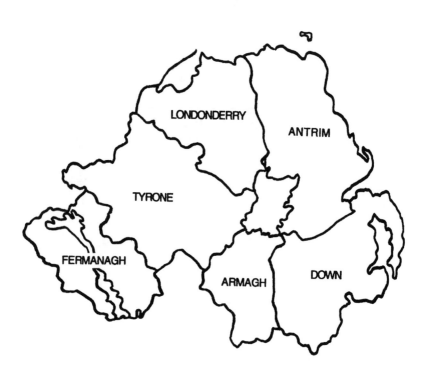

Introduction to Northern Ireland

BACKGROUND

One cannot really speak of Northern Ireland as being separate from the Republic. There are so many traditions, common heritages, and histories that bind these countries and people together. Currently, there is a genuine, common hope for peace and future prosperity on both sides of the border. We are encouraged by recent developments that reveal that the Unionists and the Republicans in the North are moving ahead to build a lasting peace.

One need not be afraid. Northern Ireland is presently very peaceful with a few isolated incidents, none of which threatened life or limb. The people are exceptionally warm, friendly, and helpful. You should not hesitate to visit Ulster. It is perfectly safe! It's like an Irish country with a British mix of customs, currency, and culture—a hybrid of sorts. This gives Northern Ireland its own interesting charm. You will be impressed by the romantic beauty of the Glens of Antrim where the mountains roll down to the sea, which hides crescent-shaped sandy swimming beaches and spectacular vistas. At one bed and breakfast on a hill above Cushendall we could look across the Irish Sea and see the Mull of Kintyre, part of Scotland—15 miles away!

One should be cautious of generalizing about the Northern Irish. You find here two predominant groups: the Irish catholics, a minority in Ulster; and the Scots and English, who are most numerous. The Scots brought their Protestant religion with them, which in most cases is rooted in Presbyterianism. The English traditionally belong to the Church of England, which is Episcopalian. This religious difference was thought by many to be at the heart of the conflict in Northern Ireland, but there have been some convincing arguments that a criminal element has benefited from the troubles through drug dealing and gun running. The United States has strongly supported programs in both Eire and the North to curb the radicals on both sides by offering economic assistance to create jobs, especially in Belfast and Londonderry. One is struck by the irony of seeing the beautiful

Ulster cities and countryside and imaging this place as a batttle-ground.

We recommend the book cited in our "Introduction to Ireland" at the beginnning of this book, Edmund Curtis' *A History of Ireland*,if you wish to explore the roots of this problem in more depth. His is one of the most popular and authoritative historical accounts up through 1922. It will help you to understand the difficulties the Irish face in achieving a lasting peace.

We found the operators of B&Bs in the North to be more conservative and cautious. While all were very friendly, we don't know if their reluctance to be in our book was due to their business acumen or because of the troubles they have endured since the early 1970s. We must explain that when we asked the hosts if they wanted to be in the book after we had inspected the premises, it took a lot more explaining than it did in the Republic of Ireland. We attribute some of this to the rapid changes occuring in people's lives in Northern Ireland. Northern Ireland does not have a *national* Town and Country Homes Association like the Republic of Ireland does. Tourism is organized more by region and county. When we were last in Londonderry, the Northern Ireland Tourist Board branch office was out of copies of a helpful booklet describing coastal B&Bs, The Town & Seaside House Association's "Be Our Special Guest," which mainly covers Down, Antrim, and Londonderry. The flood of tourists has been somewhat overwhelming.

We deeply appreciate the help from the Northern Ireland Tourist Board representatives in New York, Belfast, and Londonderry. We encourage you to avail yourself of their booking service. We found the staff in Belfast extremely courteous and welcoming. At their city or regional centers, maps, county guides, and event calendars are free. Also quality gifts, slide sets, audiotapes, and the like are available for a nominal price. For information in the U.S. call 1 (800) 326-0036 in New York; in Canada, 1 (416) 925-6368 in Toronto. There is an office in Dublin at 16 Nassau St., near the Blarney Woolen Mill shop. The Belfast office, which we found very useful, is at 59 North St. Telephone: 01232-246609. Park in the major car park nearby and walk there. People will be happy to direct you.

PRACTICAL MATTERS

We urge you to review our general advice on travel in the "Introduction to Ireland" at the beginning of the book. We won't repeat it here. These tips and advice apply as well to traveling in Northern Ireland. We have followed the same procedure and used the same standards in the North for the selection of B&Bs. Let us point out a few of the differences you can expect when you cross the border and give you some tips and advice to make your trip a great success.

Money and Changing Currency

Changing money can be a hassle, but it needn't be if you obtain American Express traveler's checks made out in pounds sterling. Most American Automobile Association offices have these for members free of charge at a reasonable exchange rate. By doing this you avoid running to a bank to exchange dollar traveler's checks and finding them closed. Our advice if you are going to tour both the South and the North, use both dollar traveler's checks in the South and sterling checks in the North. You won't be able to buy traveler's checks in Irish pounds (or punts) in the U.S.

Rental Cars

Some car rental companies do not allow you to take their car from the Republic of Ireland across the border. Check this out with your travel agent or your car rental company. Again remember Master-Card only provides you with collision insurance for 15 days overseas if you waive the insurance offered by the rental company. VISA Gold covers you for 30 days, a definite advantage if you are contemplating longer trips. Also as in the South, you drive on the opposite side of the road than you do in the U.S. Don't worry; it is easy and you will catch onto it in one day. We also find that automatic shifting is very helpful in reducing driving fatigue and in increasing ease of driving.

Booking Ahead

It is advisable to call ahead to book your next B&B stay. Most hosts will have recommendations for other B&Bs and might even call ahead for you. You can purchase a CALLCARD (or Phonecard) as in the South. These are not interchangeable with those in the Republic of Ireland. You have to buy a Northern one at the post office or some convenience stores. The rooms are priced per person unless otherwise noted. A single person will usually pay a higher rate. Currently many B&Bs are fully booked in the peak season. In June 1995, we couldn't find one room in Belfast within a reasonable price range. Northern Ireland has become a very popular tourist destination, so getting rooms in the better B&Bs like the ones in this book can be very difficult. That's why we urge you to make reservations ahead if you can.

Rooms

Almost all of the other routines in B&Bs in Northern Ireland are the same as in the Republic of Ireland. You will see the abbreviation

H&C in some listings. It means that there is a vanity or sink with a mirror in the room with hot and cold water. This allows you to wash up and brush your teeth without going to a shared bath. We bring light bathrobes and slippers for the shared bath when we occupy a standard room. These accommodations are generally cheaper than the rooms with a private bath. Frank likes the bigger mirror and sink in the shared bath when shaving, plus some shared baths have much larger showers or tub/showers than the baths en suite. We found the standards of both town and country homes and farm B&Bs in Northern Ireland to be excellent. We can't wait to go back to stay at some we could only visit for our usual interview and inspection. The rates are about the same, varying with the exchange rate of the English pound sterling instead of the Irish punt.

County Antrim

Antrim, on the northeast coast of Ulster, has majestic mountains that sweep down across grassy, green farm fields to the sea's edge, where rugged cliffs, white sandy beaches, and picturesque fishing villages form the boundary to the salty sea. The patchwork-quilt pattern of many shades of green and the man-made rock walls and farm fields complements the rest of the natural beauty and rivals those great

221

vistas we have seen in the southwest of the Republic of Ireland and those in Cape Breton, Nova Scotia, or Hawaii. There are nine scenic glens to explore. Ulster's coastal outline on a map looks like a mirror image of the coast of Scotland—a mere 15 miles away. It is here you will also find many of Scottish ancestry; these are descendants of the Scots who migrated to Northern Ireland in hopes of finding a better life.

You can start at either end of the Antrim coast road and motor east from Portstewart or northwest from the Norman town of Carrickfergus and follow the rugged coast, up and down the high mountains and then down to the water's edge with a nice swimming beach at Cushendall. The beaches are safe, clean, and uncrowded—ideal for a day at the seaside. Many towns have seaside paths for hiking. The small ports will provide fishing trips and day cruises. Rathlin Island is a bird sanctuary that draws birders from all over the world to see the Razorbill colonies and other rare species. You can book a boat trip to Rathlin Island at Ballycastle and even stay at the island's sole B&B, the Rathlin Guest House. Horseback riding, golf, forest parks and farm museums, and many other recreational activities are available. In addition to the unique experience of exploring castles and ancient tombs and churches, we particularly enjoyed the 12th-century castle at Carrickfergus on the Belfast Lough, where full-sized mannequins dressed in armour or period garb adorn the walls and rooms and give more dimension to the visit. You can also see the Slemish Mountain at Broughshane, where St. Patrick is reputed to have herded swine as a slave after he was captured and brought to Ireland from England in the fifth century.

Legends abound in Irish history. Antrim has the Giant's Causeway with its story of the giant Finn MacCool and his walk to Scotland on the unusual rock formation that continues under the sea and rises out of the sea in Scotland. Another fun visit is a walk on the Carrick-a Rede Rope Bridge, high above the beach and ocean below, located 5 miles northwest of Ballycastle. There is Waterworld for the kids at Portrush and for us older folks, in the village of Bushmills, the Old Bushmill Distillery to liven your spirits. As you can see, there is much to do and see in Antrim.

Beech Grove
Dettie and Jack Barron
412 Upper Rd., Trooper's Lane
Carrickfergus, County Antrim BT38 8PW
Telephone: 01960-363304
Bedrooms: 7; 2 with private baths, 5 with shared.
Rates: £16-18, both singles and doubles; discounts for children. £10 dinner. Vouchers accepted. **Credit cards:** None. **Open:** All year. **Children:** All ages. **Pets:** Yes. **Smoking:** Yes. **Provision for handicapped:** None. **Directions:** From Belfast, travel north for 10 miles on A2. Just left of the security wall is Trooper's Lane; follow that until you are 3 miles south of Carrickfergus. Take a right after the four lanes start. The B&B is on the left.

Beech Grove is a 1790s farmhouse just outside the famed town of Carrickfergus. It has wonderful views to the front of Belfast Lough where ships from Liverpool and the Seacat from Scotland can be seen. Jack still keeps numerous chickens and will proudly show them to you and offer to sell you some of their eggs. The seven rooms are clean and tastefully decorated in soft colors. Our room had a double and a single bed with wide pink-and-white striped coverlets, a TV, a bureau with a mirror, and extra tables (which are sometimes hard to find in Ireland). All have tea services and views of farmlands and the lake. Dettie Barron serves a lovely Irish Breakfast with choice of eggs and all kinds of breads and jams. Her table settings and dishes are attractive. Belfast, with its historic buildings, arts, drama, and museums, isn't far away to the south. You may enjoy the castle in Carrickfergus with mannequins dressed as knights and ladies on horseback, the Ulster Walk in the countryside, ferries, fishing, golf, and horseback riding. In town the children will especially enjoy the Knight's Ride, an attraction that tells the history of the area.

Culbidagh House
Roisin and Charlie Hamel
115 Red Bay Rd.
Cushendall, County Antrim BT44 0SH
Telephone: 012667-71312
Bedrooms: 3; 2 with private baths, 1 private not en suite.
Rates: £16; 50 percent discount for children under 12. Vouchers not accepted. **Credit cards:** None. **Open:** April 1 to October 30. **Children:** All ages. **Pets:** Outside only. **Smoking:** No. **Provision for handicapped:** Yes. **Directions:** Take the coast road (A8) to Cushendall. As you come into town, look for the Culbidagh House sign on the left just after the park on the right. Turn left and you will see Red Bay Boats, Ltd., on your right. Follow this street up to the top and turn left on Kilnadore Road. Go about a ½ mile; the street turns sharply right up the hill and becomes Red Bay Road. The Hamels' home is on your right about a ½ mile farther.

This home has one of the most spectacular views in all of Northern Ireland. It is snuggled high on the hillside and overlooks sweeping green fields dotted with cows and grazing sheep, the town, and the Irish Sea far below. You can see the mountains of Scotland off in the northeast. One large room offers 2 double beds; another a double and single, what the Irish call a family room; and a third is at the front with table and chairs and a spectacular view. Charming Roisin and Charles work together to prepare your breakfast at a table in front of the bay windows with the panoramic view. They offer a delicious Irish Breakfast with choices of eggs, ham, sausage, fresh fruit, cereal, juice, and coffee or tea. Although there are golf, fishing, boating, and other water sports at the beach and park, we chose to hike along the Cliff

Walk to the left of the beach and do some photography. The swimming was tempting as Ireland was experiencing a heat wave when we were there. Fran got up early one morning and attempted to scale the green-covered mountain top off to one side of the property. She made it through several sheep pastures and above until even the house looked small in the distance below. The photos she took of fields, mist, and the sea below are prize winners. The evening's entertainment is watching the sunset and the mountains change color to red and rosy pink. It stays light until almost 10:30 P.M. during the summer because the North Pole is tilted toward the sun; but the temperature stays in the balmy, high 70s or 80s.

Mountain View
Mrs. Brigid O'Neill
1 Kilnadore Rd.
Barrack Brae
Cushendall, County Antrim BT44 0SG
Telephone: 021667-71246
Bedrooms: 3, all en suite.
Rates: £13; discount for children. Vouchers accepted. **Credit cards:** None. **Open:** All year. **Children:** Yes, over 12. **Pets:** No. **Smoking:** Restricted to lounge. **Provision for handicapped:** None. **Directions:** Driving north on A2, turn left at RUC (police) station. Mountain View is the first house on the left.

One of the most colorful and dazzling gardens in Ireland greets you as you enter this 1870s home. We had to take many photographs to record the beautiful sight. Someone spends a lot of time creating this masterpiece. You'll find this bed and breakfast squeaky clean, bright, and well organized. The dining room with red drapes and matching rug is laid out with separate tables and table settings. In addition to the full Irish Breakfast, Mrs. O'Neill offers homemade potato bread, pancakes, homegrown tomatoes (in season), and fresh-brewed coffee. All three rooms view the rugged Antrim coast, the mountains, or the sea. Two rooms have brass beds; all have flowered puffs and private baths. This home is in the Cushendall Conservation Area with many restaurants, pubs, and stores within walking distance. In fact, this pretty little town is fun to walk around in, with its humpy bridge and stream and medieval "prison" at the main intersection. We liked having afternoon coffee at the bakery on the main street, and Frank liked to get the *London Financial Times* at the Spar grocery store to keep up on world events. Plan to spend at least a couple days in Cushendall!

Ballymagarry Country House
Alyson Leckey
Leeke Road
Portrush, County Antrim BT56 8NH
Telephone: 01265-823737; **FAX:** 01265-822542
Bedrooms: 4, all with private baths.
Rates: From £25 p.p. to £40; Single £40. Discount for children under twelve. **Credit cards:** VISA, Access, MasterCard. **Open:** From spring to autumn. **Children:** All ages. **Pets:** No. **Smoking:** No. **Provision for handicapped:** Yes. **Directions:** Take the coast road to Dunluce Castle from Portrush. Turn right onto Ballytober Road. Take another right onto Ballymagarry Road and then a left onto Leeke Road, or call owner.

Mrs. Alyson Leckey keeps an extraordinarily beautiful home on an ancient site with ruins of a castle and other buildings still on the grounds. This award-winning 17th-century home would rival some of the top hotels. Ballymagarry means "land of the enclosed garden" and the 16th-century walled garden is still there. Some of the rooms overlook this garden, breathtaking views of the Glens of Antrim, the mountains of Donegal, or the ocean and peaceful countryside. The luxury rooms are fresh, spacious, and modern with soothing colors and pine furniture and woodwork. All have TVs and tea facilities with homemade biscuits (cookies). Relax in "The Barn," a very large and magnificent living room, recently converted from a building that dates from 1588, with real oak beams possibly from a sunken Spanish Armada ship and a huge arched fireplace that is lit in summer and winter. The children may play in a special outdoor area as well as an indoor playroom. Breakfast, which has won a Galtee Award, is tempting with freshly squeezed orange juice, freshly ground coffee, porridge, freshly baked croissants, and a smoked salmon omelet—a specialty. The dining room was brightly lit by the sun when we were there because of the large windows on three sides. This raised area provides guests with fashionable glass-topped and wrought-iron tables with matching chairs. For sights and recreation, the Giant's Causeway, a golf course, Leisure Center, and Waterworld are very close by. Walk to Dunluce Castle or beautiful Whiterocks Beach. The Leckeys will pack a Victorian picnic for your outings. It is wise to call ahead here because they are often full.

Maddybenny Farm House (and Riding Centre)
Rosemary White
Off Loguestown Road
Portrush, County Antrim BT52 2PT
Telephone: 02165-823394
Bedrooms: 3, all with private baths; 6 self-catering cottages (4-star rated by NITB)
Rates: £25 p.p. bed and breakfast; 30 percent discount for children. Vouchers not accepted. Write to Rosemary for details on cottage rentals. **Credit cards:** VISA and MasterCard. **Open:** All year except Christmas and New Year's. **Children:** Yes, all ages. **Pets:** No. **Smoking:** Yes, except dining room. **Provision for handicapped:** None. **Directions:** Coming south from Portrush follow the sign at Magherabuoy Hotel crossroads; from Coleraine north, follow signs on A29 at Magherabuoy road and Loguestown road roundabout.

This award-winning home has been recommended to us by many friends in Ireland. It is a plantation-period farmhouse built before 1650 by the earl of Antrim and completely renovated and furnished in fine family antiques. The breakfasts have won the All Ireland "Galtee Best Farmhouse Breakfast" award in 1989, 1992, and 1994. Before you turn in, Rosemary White asks that you read the menu and write down your order for the next morning. This will be your ticket to a gourmet and delicious breakfast. For example, the porridge can be taken with Drambuie, honey, and cream. From there you select 12 main dishes. Bedrooms are large and all en suite, with color TV, each capable of sleeping 4 people. Other amenities include hospitality trays in rooms, refrigerator use in the hall for keeping your drinks and picnic things, pay phone in the hall, irons and ironing boards, and hairdryers and hot brushes. You also have full use of the cross-country and riding facilities and game room. Mrs. White can direct you to local gourmet restaurants, Giant's causeway, golf courses, and other tourist sites.

ALSO RECOMMENDED

Belfast, *Oakhill Country House,* May Noble, 59 Dunmurry Lane BT17 9JR. Telephone: 0232-610658. FAX: 0232-621566. Bedrooms: 4, 3 en suite. Luxury country home 4 miles from Belfast. Amazing gardens and extraordinarily charming interior. Large baths. No pets. Breakfast served in the conservatory during the summer months.

Dundonald, *The Cottage,* Mrs. Elizabeth Muldoon, 377 Comber St., Belfast BT16 0XB. Telephone: 0247-878189. Bedrooms: 3, all with shared bath. Bedrooms are small but this is a home remodeled from a 1740s cottage. Delightful with lots of character and attractively landscaped. 3 miles east of Belfast on the A20.

Portrush, *Royal Court Hotel,* 233 Ballybogy Rd., Ballymagarry. Off A2 where you turn to Ballymoney a few miles east of Portrush. Telephone: 01265-822236. A luxury hotel under new management, where we enjoyed many meals while in the area. Ultra-luxurious doubles with canopy bed and tiled baths, some with views of the ocean. There is an ocean-facing suite with 2 bedrooms and living room with large TV plus dining room that could be used for conferences. Nice for a family seeking luxury hotel accommodations in this popular resort. Meals were great but service was slow when we were there. The doubles are a good value as far as hotel prices go.

Portrush, *White Rocks,* Mrs. E. Allen, Prop. 105 Dunluce Rd. BT56 8NB. Telephone: 01265-823407. Bedrooms: 5, 2 en suite. Open all year. Faces the dunes and ocean. Quiet chalet bungalow.

COUNTY ARMAGH

County Armagh

Armagh, the smallest of Northern Ireland counties, reaches from Louth in the south to Lough Neagh and Tyrone in the north and is bordered by Monaghan to the west. Again, gentle hills and quiet farms abide. Saint Patrick called the county "my sweet hill."

The capitol city of Armagh is the most venerated of Irish cities, and the Roman Catholic Cathedral and the Protestant Church of Ireland Cathedral have been sitting on hills, facing each other, since the mid-1800s. This is where Ulster kings reigned hundreds of years ago and where the great Brian Boru is buried. You'll find this a sophisticated, comfortable old city with many trees, fine Georgian brick houses, iron gates and lampposts, and a wide green mall for walking and games. There is a fusiliers museum on the Mall.

Visit the great Observatory, built by Archbishop Robinson, Saint Patrick's Trian, the Palace Stables, and historic houses such as The Argory and the Ardress House. Two miles southwest of Armagh, see the raised, circular Navan Fort, and Celtic crosses. Farther south, towards Newry on the A25, is a 1700s thatched manor house, Derrymore, with a large park of 48 acres for you to visit.

Northeast of Armagh Town in the Bramley apple-growing country, the sweet aroma of apple blossoms fill the air in May. At the end of October, a celebration of Apple Harvest is held, with hundreds of spicy, warm apple pies, freshly baked and served with thick cream. Summers in Armagh bring sheep dog trials, terrier races, and gun-dog scurries.

In Armagh, a popular game is "Road Bowls," where men compete throwing a metal ball down country roads to see how far it will go. Armagh men often win the Irish Championships, which are held at different places each year, all over the North and South of Ireland. On one of our visits to Blarney, the road to our B&B was closed for the play-offs of Road Bowls.

Deans Hill
Mrs. Jill Armstrong
College Hill
Armagh Town, County Armagh BT61 9DF
Telephone: 01861-524923
Bedrooms: 3, 2 with private baths, 1 with shared. H&C in all rooms.
Rates: £25; Single £20; negotiable discount for children. Vouchers not accepted. **Credit cards:** None. **Open:** All year, except Christmas. **Children:** All ages. **Pets:** Inquire of Mrs. Armstrong. **Smoking:** Restricted. **Provision for handicapped:** None. **Directions:** Driving out of Armagh Centre on A3 toward Portadown, Deans Hill is the first stone entrance on the left avenue after Tower Hill after the Armargh Planetarium and Observatory and before the filling station and roundabout.

Built in 1772, Deans Hill has been in the Armstrong family since 1880 and has retained its elegance and charm as a Victorian country home. Guest accommodations are centrally heated and include large comfortable bedrooms with their original features and period decorations, including one four-poster bedroom and a twin bedroom with an open fireplace. Guests can relax in a cozy sitting room with a TV and an open fire. Breakfast is served in the dining room and includes a full Irish Breakfast with homemade jams and eggs fresh from the farm. Deans Hill is set in wooded grounds with a tennis court and croquet lawn and has a working farm at your disposal to visit. It is also surprisingly close, only a ten-minute walk, to historic Armagh Town with its famous Georgian architecture, St. Patrick's Cathedral, the Mall, the County Museum, and the Regimental Museum. Also watch the cricket match being played on a fine green. Nearby are the famous Planetarium and Conservatory, good restaurants, and interesting shops. Most sporting activities are available locally: riding, fishing, and golf. Several interesting National Trust properties are within minutes. The Navan Fort, one of the most interesting archeological sites in Ireland because of its mix of factual archeology, myths, and legends, is a 5-minute drive away. Armagh is also an excellent center for genealogical research.

Redbrick Country House
Moreen Stephenson
Corbrackey Lane
Portadown, County Armagh BT62 1PQ
Telephone: 01762-335268
Bedrooms: 7; 3 with private baths, 4 with shared.
Rates: £16 p.p.; light supper included in price. Vouchers not accepted.
Credit cards: None. **Open:** All year. **Children:** All ages. **Pets:** No. **Smoking:** Restricted. **Provision for handicapped:** None. **Directions:** First-time visitors will be met by appointment.

This modern country home is set in quiet, secluded, rolling farmland and is centarally located so you can drive to any part of the province in less than two hours. Moreen, a friendly hostess, will help you plan your trip and enjoy the area. The bedrooms are tastefully decorated and comfortable. A full Irish Breakfast is served in the country kitchen. Tea and coffee welcome you on arrival. This bed and breakfast is close to golf, water sports, shooting, and Lough Neagh, and the Armagh Heritage Centre. Moreen prides herself on the warm welcome and the family atmosphere.

COUNTY DOWN

County Down

County Down borders on the Republic of Ireland, where people get their first glimpse of the North coming from Dublin and eastern areas. It presents wonderful first views of rolling green hills, wooden fences, and wide roads. Newry, the first pretty town you'll visit, has an excellent little tourist bureau right in the Town Hall at the bridge in the town's center. Here you can also visit the Newry Arts Centre and Museum. At the head of Carlingford Lough, Newry is mostly a farm town, and you'll see the grazing sheep and cows very soon after you leave the town center. To the southeast, the stately purple Mourne Mountains can be seen for miles.

If you head for the seaside, you'll take the A2, or the coast road, to lovely Kilkeel, where you can enjoy the beaches, watch fishing boats, and visit Green Castle. Going north to Newcastle, you'll pass Donard Cave and Maggie's Leap. In the port of Newcastle, walk the promenade or go swimming, boating, or ponytrekking along the beach. You can camp at Tollymore Forest Park, where there is a great wildlife reserve.

Downpatrick is a fascinating area, with the cathedral overlooking the Quoile River, and the stone grave of Saint Patrick. This is where Saint Patrick lived out his last days in A.D. 46. You may want to visit the ruins of Saint Tassach's Church near Saul, where he took his last Holy Communion. Cross over to Portaferry and the peninsula of beauty along Strangford Lough. Greyabbey has not only the famed Grey Abbey, but it is an "antique heaven." Farther north, visit the charming Mount Stewart House and acres of gardens on the way to Newtownards. Strangford Lough, which opens out to the sea, is so large it would be called a bay in America. These towns along the water's edge have gorgeous beaches and views.

From Newtownards you're only a half-hour from Belfast, if you drive during the midday. Here you'll find an astonishing city with many Victorian buildings that hearken back to the days of linen-making and shipbuilding. There are some boarded-up windows, but you'd hardly notice that fighting and guns used to be the order of the day.

They've done some lavish reconstruction of the downtown area with many streets closed off to all traffic but shopping buses. Well-known storefronts of classy design line these streets, and it's safe to walk anywhere since peace has been established. Visit the huge, glittering multistoried shopping mall called Castlecourt Centre that is off Royal Avenue. The wonderful Northern Irish Tourist Bureau, situated in the town center at 59 North St., will give you help in all directions. Sheila Cameron and Maureen Campbell were especially tireless and very generous with their attention to us. Their phone number is 01232 or 0-800-317153 (credit cards only).

Not far away at the end of High Street is the famed Albert Memorial Clock Tower and the Anglican St. Anne's Cathedral. We enjoyed a delicious and reasonable lunch at the handsome Deer's Head Pub across from the Tourist Board. Other good pubs are White's Tavern, built in 1630, and the famous Victorian Crown Liquor Saloon at 46 Great Victoria St. One B&B owner sent us for an excellent Italian meal to Gigolo's Restaurant at 23 Donegal Pass Rd. Not only does the charming owner come out of the kitchen to explain his splendid recipes, but at night he'll serenade you with Italian arias. Visit the rococo Grand Opera House on Great Victoria Street with all of its gold trim. Here they hold plays, musical operas, and a children's theater. The Lyric Theater also has plays and music. In November, the Belfast Arts Festival at Queen's University has hundreds of cultural events. Don't pass up a tour of the grand old City Hall with its lovely marble inside. Of course, you'll want to see the beautiful Botanic Gardens.

If you were to continue north on the A24 from Downpatrick, you'd reach the historic town of Ballynahinch with its wide streets. It was the scene of a battle in 1798, where 7,000 United Irishmen died trying to take the city. Go southwest from this town to see Northern Ireland's best known Neolithic dolmen, the Legananny, with its large delicately balanced stones.

Bushymead Country House
Mrs. Sally Murphy
86 Drumaness Rd.
Ballynahinch, County Down BT24 8LT
Telephone: 01238-561171
Bedrooms: 10; 7 with private baths, 3 with shared.
Rates: £16-12 p.p. private bath; £13-16 shared; discount for children.
Vouchers accepted. £8-13 dinner. **Credit cards:** Yes. **Open:** January to
December. **Children:** All ages. **Pets:** Yes. **Smoking:** No. **Provision for
handicapped:** Yes, but not wheelchairs. **Directions:** South of Belfast on
the A24, continue south from Ballynahinch Square for about 2 miles
toward Drumaness and Newcastle. Bushy-mead is on the left. Coming
from Drumaness on A24, look for the Bushymead sign on your right,
about 2 miles before Ballynahinch Square.

This lovely and luxurious country home surrounded by pretty gardens, set in the heart of Down, has received high recommendations
from travelers all over the world. It is at the gateway to Newcastle and
the Mourne Mountains. All rooms are colorfully decorated with the
decor highlighted in period style furnishings, some with antique fireplaces and beds with partial canopies. All rooms have tea- and coffee-
making facilities. Some have color TVs. A separate guest lounge is
available for friendly chats. Breakfast is a tasty full Irish one, and meals
are available all day. There is a small fitness suite and a children's
playground with pet animals, so one can see this is an unusual B&B
when you consider all the amenities. Golf, fishing, museums, and forest parks are nearby, so this would make an excellent base camp for
exploring County Down. They recently won the award of "Best for
Guests."

The Old Rectory
Mary Callan
148 Malone Rd.
Belfast, County Down BT9 5LH
Telephone: 01232-667882
Bedrooms: 4, all with private baths. New rooms under construction.
Rates: £55 p.p.; Single £39; discount for children. Vouchers not accepted. **Credit cards:** None. **Open:** All year, except Christmas and Easter. **Children:** All ages. **Pets:** No. **Smoking:** Restricted. **Provisions for handicapped:** None. **Directions:** Follow University Road from Belfast, past Queen's University. University Road becomes Malone Road. The Old Rectory is 1.5 miles farther on the lefthand side; look for the numbers on the left.

As the name implies, The Old Rectory was the home to the minister of St. John's Parish and was built in 1896. This luxury B&B still has some views of the Belfast Mountains, even though it's handy to the town center of Belfast. The four large rooms are beautifully furnished in pastel shades of green and rose, and all have TVs and tea-making facilities. One room has a liberty print and an old pine trim. A complimentary hot whiskey is served in the fireplaced drawing room every evening at 9:30. Mary's husband Jerry is a professional chef and makes a hearty Irish breakfast, which sometimes offers croissants and other surprises. There is always fresh orange juice, fresh fruit, cheese, and yogurts. The home is only two miles out of town, very handy to good shops, restaurants, pubs, walking tours, The Ulster Museum, Botanical Garden, and golf. Visit the countryside in County Antrim to the north and County Down to the south.

Hillside Guesthouse
Jackie McNally
1 Rock Road Tormore
Newry, County Down BT34 1PL
Telephone: 01693-65484
Bedrooms: 6; 3 with private baths, 3 with shared baths—sinks in the room and the bathroom next door.
Rates: £16 p.p.; Single £18; discount for children. Babysitting services available. Vouchers not accepted. Registered with the Northern Ireland Tourist Bureau. **Credit cards:** None. **Open:** All year. **Children:** All ages. **Pets:** No. **Smoking:** Restricted. **Provision for handicapped:** Yes. **Directions:** It is less than a 10-minute drive from Newry, going north on Belfast Road (M1). The road is on right just *before* the sign for Hillside Guesthouse.

Jackie McNally runs this new 6-room bed and breakfast in the middle of beautiful farm lands and rolling hills. Most of the rooms have gorgeous views of cow pastures and hills with mountains in the distance. They are good sized and decorated in pink and apricot colors. In the morning from our lovely room, we heard cows mooing in a pasture below. Jackie serves a full Irish Breakfast with a choice of eggs and she likes to chat with her guests. She offers a "baby listening" service. Fran took a walk up the steep road behind the house and enjoyed the wonderful views of farm after farm. It was very tranquil and gratifying. You'll find fishing and bowling nearby, and the seaside is just 15 minutes away. There is a good restaurant and pub just down the road. Jackie said that they may open up 10 more rooms plus a restaurant if the "peace" holds. The bustling city of Belfast is only a half-hour away.

Edenvale House
Diane and Gordon Whyte
130 Portaferry Rd.
Newtownards, County Down BT22 2AH
Telephone: 01247-814881; **FAX:** 01247-826192
Bedrooms: 3 with private baths.
Rates: £25; Single £30. Vouchers not accepted. **Credit cards:** Yes.
Open: January 20 to December 20. **Children:** All ages. **Pets:** Yes. **Smoking:** Restricted to sunroom. **Provision for handicapped:** Only if they can manage stairs. **Directions:** It is on the east side of Strangford Lough, about 2 miles south of the town of Newtonards and the Flying Club on the Belfast-Portaferry Road (A20). Before the stone pillar entrance, there is a large "Butterlump Rock" on the beach to your right and a row of cottages on your left. The small Edenvale House sign at the entrance on the left is easy to miss. It is before Mount Stewart Garden. *A note of caution:* This is a dangerous entrance when leaving; enter the road slowly.

This elegant 1780 Georgian house is a part of a seven-acre farm, and Diane and Gordon Whyte keep six horses but not for riding. Stables are available *free* for horses or dogs. Mrs. Whyte gave us a friendly full Irish welcome with a tea and delicious strawberry tarts on the patio outside the sunroom. From here we had a perfect view across the Lough to the Mourne Mountains. Their two dogs, Badger and Nip—one large, one small—will greet you as well. The three rooms in this beautifully renovated home are all carpeted with large, tastefully decorated baths. Antiques grace all of the rooms. One has a large, canopied, king-sized bed with soft green and pink decor; another is pale blue and yellow. The living room is roomy and the country kitchen with hanging herbs is sunny and inviting. This B&B looks like something out of *House Beautiful* or *Home and Garden* magazines. Their breakfast of hot homemade breads, fried potato bread, and hot fruit compote with cream along with the traditional Irish Breakfast will not be forgotten. Places to visit in the area are the world-famous Mount Stewart Garden and Estate, antique shops in Greyabbey, and Castle Espie Wildlife Centre. For the sports-minded there is sailing, wind surfing, riding, and bird watching.

ALSO RECOMMENDED

Ardglass, *The Strand Farm,* Mrs. Mary Donovan, 231 Arglass Rd. BT30 7UL. Telephone: 0396-841446. Bedrooms: 2. Open all year. Secluded farmhouse in peaceful surroundings. Home baking. Children's pony and trap.

Bangor, *Hebron House,* The Maddock family, 59 Queens Parade BT20 3BH. Telephone: 01247-463126. Bedrooms: 3. A Victorian listed home overlooking Bangor Marina. Open all year. Recommended by our friend, Helen Callanan, a B&B owner from Dún Laoghaire.

Belfast, *Camera House,* Paul and Angela Drumm, 44 Wellington Park BT9 6DP. Telephone: 01232-660026. Bedrooms: 11, all with baths and TVs. No credit cards. Lovely red-bricked Victorian-styled house near city center. Highly recommended.

Groomsport, *Tanner Cottage,* Mrs. L. Walker, 5 Main St. Telephone: 0247-46534. Bedrooms: 2, both en suite. Open all year. A lovely home, east of Bangor. Many amenities.

Kilkeel, *Kilmorey Arms Hotel,* Prop: Mrs. McMurray, 41-43 Greencastle St. Telephone: 016937-622220 or 62801. Bedrooms: 26, all en suite. Discount for seniors. Evening meal available. Delightful small inn with homey atmosphere. Worth the extra money. Nice cocktail lounge and public bar, worthy of a pint or two if passing through Kilkeel, or if you're thirsty from a walk in the Mournes.

Newry, *Ashton House,* Mrs. Bridget Heaney, 37 Omeath Rd., Fathom Line BT35 8QW. Telephone: 01693-62120. Bedrooms 8, all en suite. Pretty 18th-century home situated on 22 acres of farmland overlooking Newry canal on the main scenic route to Carlingford and the Cooley Mountains.

COUNTY FERMANAGH

County Fermanagh

County Fermanagh is a region of rolling hills and farms, but Lough Erne and its upper and lower loughs with its enchanting and historic islands dominate the region. And where the lake and inland waterway appear pinched off in the middle stands the ancient town of Enniskillen. Plan to spend some time here and revel in the beauty of the lakes and mystical and enchanting quality of the ancient tales. Many a struggle for control of this strategic town was fought here. In those medieval times when there was peace, you can almost imagine the lords and ladies gathering at Enniskillen Castle for dinner and poetry reading after the men returned from the hunt.

This restored castle keep and barracks is a must for its display of past life in this region, its natural history, regimental museum, and a room dedicated to the life and work of a famous porcelain artist from Enniskillen. Also, while at the castle, be sure to view the excellent videos on the second floor of the museum that tell the story of Enniskillen past and present and the romantic stories of the Maguires who fought for and against the British. The Buttermarket is now a craft center where you can buy lace, knitwear, and Belleek china. To see this distinctive porcelain being made, go to Belleek Village, 25 miles away where the Erne rushes to meet the Atlantic.

South of Enniskillen on the A4 is Castle Coole, a splendid neoclassical mansion set on the shore of Lough Coole and surrounded by a parkland. Also the 18th-century, three-story manor home, Florence Court, about 8 miles southwest of Enniskillen via the A4 and A32, is another place you must visit. For those interested in caves and cool places, the Marble Arch Caves near Florence Court, which are reported to be one of the most awesome sights in Europe, provide you with a boat ride and all the spectacles associated with large underground cave systems. Call ahead for an update on current hours of operation (Telephone: 01365-348855). For horse and equestrian fans there is the Ulster Equestrian Centre at Necarne, Irvinestown (Telephone: 013656-21919).

Lackaboy Farm
Mrs. Derrick Noble
Tempo Road
Enniskillen, County Fermanagh BT74 6EB
Telephone: 01365-322488
Bedrooms: 7; 4 with private baths, 3 with shared.
Rates: £15 p.p. private bath; £14 p.p. shared bath; Single £18; discount for children. Vouchers accepted. £10 dinner (4 courses). **Credit cards:** VISA, Access, and AMEX. **Open:** All year, except Christmas. **Children:** All ages; baby sitting available. **Pets:** No. **Smoking:** No. **Provision for handicapped:** Yes. **Directions:** Take the B80 out of Enniskillen. Go about one mile. You'll see the guesthouse sign. Turn left and follow Tempo Road for a few hundred yards. Past a paddock and opposite the Fermanagh Agricultural Centre, you will see Lackaboy Farm on the left. It has a low, white-walled entrance that leads to the white, two-storied farmhouse.

Lackaboy Farm guesthouse is part of a dairy farm with 45 Fresian cows. Using a century-old foundation, the Nobles rebuilt the house in keeping with the character of the original home. It is notable for its Amishlike simplicity, neatness, and charm. The seven rooms are all of good size and attractive with flowered duvets and views of the farm and surrounding hills. All have H&C. For breakfast Mrs. Noble has a trolley of cereals, fruit, and cheese along with her traditional Irish Breakfast and her brewed coffee. She offers a scrumptious 4-course dinner if you book ahead. At the Agricultural Centre across the street, livestock auctions and horse shows are held. This farm is just outside historic Enniskillen, which serves as a connecting channel for the upper and lower parts of Lough Erne. Golf courses are nearby. As we walked alongside the lough in the castle park one evening after having a delicious meal at Mulligan's (33-35 Darling St.), we saw holiday seekers cruising in their rented yachts and young people practicing in their racing shells for an upcoming tournament. Ducks were swimming among the bullrushes. This was a beautiful scene that begged to be painted. This farm was recommended to us as a special place by many Northern Irish who like to come here for a week at a time.

ALSO RECOMMENDED

Enniskillen, *Ashwood Guest House,* Mrs Beryl Harris, Sligo Road. Telephone: 0365-323019. Bedrooms: 7, 4 doubles (2 en suite), 3 family or triples (2 en suite). Award-winning modern country house. Mrs. Harris is a Cordon Bleu-certified cook. Driving range and golf course next door. Near Marble Arch caves. 2 miles out of town on A4. Favorite of Northern Irish and many others.

COUNTY LONDONDERRY

County Londonderry

St. Columb came out of Donegal 1,400 years ago and founded his first monastery in the oak grove (Doire in Gaelic), a gift from his cousin, Prince of Ailech. It was a holy place. The saint said that "the angels of God sang in the glades of Derry and every leaf held its angel."

Londonderry is the second largest city in Northern Ireland and borders on Donegal. This beautiful city with its massive medieval walls and four gates perched on the banks of Lough Foyle presents a wonderful opportunity for a walking tour of the 1633 Gothic cathedral of St. Columb, the ornate Victorian Guildhall, and the many shops and pubs. We enjoyed our pub grub pints at J & T McGinleys (24 Foyle Street) after we toured the city. It is an excellent pub with character and history, formerly owned by a tea merchant. We did not see or hear of any troubles in Derry while we were in Northern Ireland, so one should not be fearful of fully enjoying the sights and sounds of this historic and scenic city.

The countryside of Derry spreads over a flat plain from the city to Limavady and Coleraine. If you take the A2 north on the west side of Limavady you will be able to complete a scenic loop of the Roe Valley and over the mountain top drive of Mt. Bineveneagh beginning on the north coast turning south at Downhill, or continue on the coastal A2 to Coleraine, past the Mussenden Temple built by an eccentric bishop of Derry as testimony of his affection for Mrs. Musssenden. The main road from Coleraine to Limavady on the A37 is equally breathtaking in its panoramic view of the valley to the west. Limavady is where Jane Ross penned the tune of the famous "Londonderry Air" ('Danny Boy'), which she heard a passing fiddler play. Another attraction is the Roe Valley Country Park 2 miles south of Limavady via the B192. A restored old linen mill and hydroelectric station built in 1896 are on the grounds with a museum. Activities at the park include canoeing, fishing, picnicking, and rock climbing. The most northeastern town in Londonderry is Portstewart, which is astride the Magilligan Strand. The longest beach in Ireland, the Magilligan Strand is formed where the Bann River empties into the Atlantic.

Ballyhenry House
Rosemary Kane
172 Seacoast Rd.
Limavady, County Londonderry BT49 9EF
Telephone: 015047-22657
Bedrooms: 3, 1 with private, 2 with shared.
Rates: £16 p.p.; Single £18; discount for children. Vouchers accepted.
Credit cards: None. **Open:** All year. **Children:** All ages. **Pets:** Outside.
Smoking: In lounge only. **Provision for handicapped:** None. **Directions:** Take the A2 from Coleraine to Limavady. As you leave Limavady headed toward Londonderry Town, you will cross the Roe River Bridge. At the end of the bridge and at the light turn right or north onto the B69. About 3.3 miles toward Downhill, you will see the colorful sign for the farm on the left. From Derry, turn left at the light at the end of the Roe River Bridge. The directions remain the same as above.

Ballyhenry House is a lovely, airy farmhouse bed and breakfast with a large, catchy, bright-colored sign featuring a farmer with a scythe. The Kane family raises seed wheat and barley and has more than 100 sheep and fifty cattle on this 1901 farm. The three bedrooms are spacious and sunny and have great pastoral views. One of the rooms was bright yellow and the one where we stayed had soothing lavender-and-blue wallpaper with matching bedspreads and wall-to-wall rugs. All have sinks in the rooms and 2 have a shared bath. One new large family room has a balcony. Rosemary Kane serves an Irish breakfast with choice of fresh fruit in season, porridge, yogurt, cereal, and teas and coffee. The house sits on a flat plain in clear veiw of the steep Binevenagh Mountain. Mrs. Kane sent us on a car ride up the 384-meter mountain, which we took in late evening after dinner, for a grand view of the mountains of Donegal, Lough Foyle to the west, and the sea to the north. We spent a long time up there watching some young men haying in the dimming light of sunset around 10:30 P.M. An enchanting and romantic sight! It's a fascinating area when you realize there is nothing else between you and the North Pole but the Hebrides and a few scattered islands. There is also golf, fishing, a Roe Valley Country Park for picnicking, walks, ponytrekking, and hang-gliding in the area. A bird sanctuary and a museum, as well as the bustling town of Limavady, are nearby. Also, the many attractions of the large city of Londonderry are not far away.

Elagh Hall
Elizabeth Buchanan
Buncrana Road
Londonderry Town, County Londonderry BT48 8LU
Telephone: 01504-263116
Bedrooms: 3; 2 with private baths, 1 with shared. **Rates:** £16 p.p. private bath; £16 p.p. shared bath; Single £17.50; 50 percent discount for children. Vouchers accepted. **Credit cards:** None. **Open:** From April to October 31. **Children:** All ages. **Pets:** No. **Smoking:** No. **Provision for handicapped:** None. **Directions:** From Londonderry, take Buncrana Road (A2) about 1½ miles, turn right at Elagh Road (the first right after the BP Station).

This 1795 farmhouse is set on 100 acres of rich farmland where the owners raise mostly sheep and cattle. This was the manse for the Burt Presbyterian Church just across the border in Donegal. It was purchased by John Buchanan's father in 1948 and it has been in the family ever since. The house is handsomely decorated with antique furniture and all of the rooms have views of either Grianan Castle or the Donegal Hills. Elizabeth offers a full Irish Breakfast, and her specialties are homemade jams (raspberry, strawberry, and black-currant from berries grown in her own garden). The house has an Old-World atmosphere, like a step back in time. You wake up in the morning to lovely fresh air, singing birds, and sheep bleating in meadows below. Templemore Sports Complex is 1 mile away; there are 2 golf courses; fishing, horseback riding, beautiful sandy beaches, are nearby. The Buchanans highly recommend Harry's restauraunt, which is not far from Elagh Hall.

Number 10
Grace and Gerry McGoldrick
No. 10 Crawford Square
Londonderry Town, County Londonderry BT48 7HR
Telephone: 01504-265000
Bedrooms: 3, all with private baths.
Rates: £17 p.p.; Single, additional charge; discount for children.
Vouchers not accepted. **Credit cards:** None. **Open:** all year. **Children:**
All ages. **Pets:** No. **Smoking:** No. **Provision for handicapped:** None.
Directions: Call ahead for directions.

Number 10 is a family-run, modernized 1890s Victorian townhouse
on three floors in unspoiled Crawford Square overlooking a park. It
is quiet here off the main street. Personable Grace McGoldrick and a
helpful lady keep it spotlessly clean. The mix of new woodwork in the
baths and the stately furnishings in the parlor give this home a special charm. The parlor has a comfy couch and chairs surrounded by
many books, paintings, and family photos. You could imagine the family gathered around the piano for a singalong. The rooms all have
pretty pastel colors, TVs, and tea- and coffee-making facilities. Grace
serves a very tasty Irish breakfast and offers a menu that includes
choices of juices, half of a grapefruit, cereals, bacon, sausage, tomato,
and eggs. A special feature is the baked kippers. This is an ideal place
to stay while visiting the many sights in this historic and beautiful city.
We recommend a walk around the 17th-century wall with its four
gates, the Tower Museum, the Guildhall, St. Columb's Cathedral, and
walking tours from the Tourist Board's office on Foyle Street. Many
Ulster Irish left Derry from the quay behind the Guildhall to emi-
grate to the New World. Try Da Vinci's Restaurant. We enjoyed its Old-
World style and service. It's reasonable, too.

Robin Hill
Malcolm and Gemma Muir
103 Chapel Road
Waterside
Londonderry Town, County Londonderry BT47 2BG
Telephone: 01504-342776; **FAX:** 01504-312776
Bedrooms: 8; 6 with private baths, 2 with shared.
Rates: £19 p.p. private bath; £16 p.p. shared; discount for children.
£9.50 dinner. **Credit cards:** None. **Open:** January to November. **Children:** Yes, all ages. **Pets:** No. **Smoking:** Some nonsmoking rooms. **Provision for handicapped:** Yes. **Directions:** From City Centre cross Craiavon Bridge to Waterside, then to Spencer Road. Second right is Fountain Hill. At the top, turn left onto Chapel Road. Take the first driveway on right. Look for the B&B sign.

A country setting in the heart of the city, Robin Hill was built as a Presbyterian manse in 1879. A Victorian-style building located on approximately one and a half acres of land on a hill with beautiful panoramic views of the city, the River Foyle, and the Donegal hills. The Muirs have lived here since 1985; Gemma is a teacher and Malcolm looks after the bed and breakfast affairs. All rooms are in warm colors, comfortable, and attractively decorated. Your hosts will serve a full "Ulster Fry" or a continental breakfast—the usual and the unusual catered for. Evening meals are available on request. There is a private car park. Londonderry Town offers walking tours and great shops—all handy to Robin Hill. River and sea angling is another recreational feature.

Ashleigh House
Margaret Gordon
Station Road
Portstewart, County Londonderry BT55 7PU
Telephone: 01265-834452
Bedrooms: 6, all with private baths.
Rates: £17-18 p.p.; discount for children under 12. Vouchers not accepted. **Credit cards:** None. **Open:** All year. **Children:** All ages. **Pets:** No. **Smoking:** Outside. **Provision for handicapped:** Yes. **Directions:** Take the A2 from Portrush to Portstewart. Just before you get into town, turn left onto Station Road, just before a large, yellow building (York Lounge). The house is about ½ mile on the right.

This modern bed and breakfast is very stylishly decorated and centers around a large, lovely garden full of peonies and roses. Margaret, a very friendly hostess, welcomed us into the warm and handsome sitting room with tea and biscuits. The six rooms are in varied colors: one has twin beds in light blue; one has a double bed with tiny pink flowers, a family room with a double bed, two twins done in apricot, and a very large bathroom. One has a large double en suite and overlooks the gardens. In the airy dining room, with pink tablecloths, which also overlooks the garden, Margaret Gordon serves a full Irish Breakfast with fresh fruit, 4 or 5 cereals, choice of eggs, tomato, or mushrooms, pancakes, and potato bread—nearly anything you want. The seaside resort of Portstewart is known for its sandy beaches and nearness to the Giant's Causeway, Dunluce Castle, and the Bushmills Brewery. The old traditional town of Limavady is nearby with its Roe Valley County Park. The famous busy city of Londonderry is only a few miles away. Ashleigh House is one we would like to visit again to spend more time!

ALSO RECOMMENDED

Coleraine, *Blackheath House,* Mrs. Erwin, 112 Killeague Rd. BT51 4HH. Telephone: 01265-868433. Bedrooms: 5, all en suite. Evening meal available. Lovely country home set in rural surroundings 7 miles south of Coleraine. Washing facilities.

Coleraine, *Camus House,* Mrs. Josephine King, 27 Curragh Rd. BT51 3RY. Telephone: 01265-2982. Bedrooms: 3 (none with bath), 1 is a triple. Joey will make you feel welcome in this quaint 1685 home. It has won House-Country awards.

County Tyrone

When we first drove up to County Tyrone from Monaghan, we were struck with the pretty green rolling hills and neat farmlands with fertile valleys. Farther north there are the majestic Sperrin Mountains, which are excellent for walks through fields with grazing sheep, yellowed in the mild winter by whin or gorse (juniper). Dyeing boiled eggs in whin to color them yellow is an Easter custom.

At Strabane you can see some special Tyrone countryside if you drive southeast on the B47 through the Sperrin Mountains to Draperstown, south on the B162 to Cookstown, and then west to Omagh on the A505—stop at a pub or two along the way to quench your thirst. Farther north from Omagh is Gortin with the Sperrin Heritage Center, where there are gold-mining and natural history exhibits, a craft shop, and a cafe. One of our favorite stops (where you will want to spend at least a half-day) is the Ulster-American Folk Park. Its main theme is the history of the 18th- and 19th-century Ulster emgration to North America. Original homes, one from the ancestors of the Mellon family (who endowed the park), are arranged in tree-lined paths and each one tells in chronological order the story of the Ulster Irish in America, the covered wagons, the sod prairie houses—even a large ship that you can board to see the appalling conditions endured by the emigrants en route to America. It is very creative and educational as well as great fun. A cafe is there at the entrance for teas and light meals.

Many Neolithic sites include the Beaghmore stone circles at Cookstown, which were uncovered only 40 years ago, and the chambered cairn of Knockmany at the top of a steep wooded hill north of Clogher. At Ardboe there is an 18-foot Celtic cross. Another Celtic feature is the 14th-century Gaelic stronghold in West Tyrone: Harry Avery's Castle. The ancestral home of Woodrow Wilson is at Strabane and his farm is still kept open by the Wilsons, who will show callers around the house. We almost lost count of the number of American presidents with Ulster roots or ancestors. Antrim has 5 alone!

Greenmount Lodge Country House
Mrs. Frances Reid
58 Greenmount Rd.
Gortaclare
Omagh, County Tyrone BT79 0YE
Telephone: 01662-841325; **FAX:** 01662-840019
Bedrooms: 8, all en suite.
Rates: £16-17.50 p.p.; Single £21; 50 percent discount for children.
£11-14 dinner. **Credit cards:** Yes. **Open:** January 1 to December 12.
Children: All ages. **Pets:** Outside. **Smoking:** No. **Provision for handicapped:** Yes, the best accommodations in the area (NITB Category 1 classification). **Directions:** Off of the A5 (or Omagh to Ballygawley Road), about 8 miles south of Omagh town or 7 miles from Ballygawley. Turn right after the Travellers Restaurant/Pub toward Beragh. The sign for Greenmount is on the left after the 4-way intersection.

This lovely Grade-A farm bed and breakfast, really a historical country estate, is set in the tranquility of 150 acres of beautiful scenery. West Tyrone is a surprising mixture of bleak, brownish boglands with whaleback hills that are separated by fertile valleys and rich pastures. Award-winning Greenmount Lodge has luxury accommodations that draw rave reviews from many guests from different countries. One guest wrote, "The host and hostess make us feel as though we are their sole guests." Their guestbook sings out "Excellent" in many languages. The guest rooms are fashionably decorated and the beds are comfortable. The full Irish Breakfast is begun with a buffet table of "starters" of various cereals, oats, fresh fruits, juices, and yogurts. Fish and vegetarian dishes are also available on request. The Reids can accommodate most dietary requirements. The "sweet table" on weekends is reputed to be the best in Ireland. Having hosted guests for 25 years, the Reids will provide you with warm hospitaliy, good food, and a relaxing atmosphere. As they are on the northwest passage, this will make an ideal "base camp" for exploring the many parks, castles, museums, and natural and historical features of the region.

Index

LODGINGS

(County in parentheses)

NORTHERN IRELAND CITIES AND TOWNS